KU-686-224

Contents

Foreword

Although the problems of famine and malnutrition do not often achieve substantial press or publicity exposure, the tragedies they represent are permanent. But they are not simple by any means.

The last few years have seen the explosions of several myths about development policy, and this is all to the good. This book explodes a few more myths, and in doing so makes a substantial contribution to our knowledge and understanding of international food policies.

Most importantly, the book focuses on developing countries, who do not need food but do need economic stimulus in order to build up their food-producing capability. My own experience in visiting several Third World countries with development needs is that an absolutely vital role is played in many of these countries by the non-governmental organisations (NGOs); these activities are particularly important and effective when the efforts of the NGOs are made in co-operation with each other. The work of Christian Aid in these respects is legendary, but most NGOs are deservedly acquiring increasing credit through their conviction that teamwork is essential in development practice.

International food policies clearly provide the heaviest influence on market prices and on the economic choices of Third World economies. The substantial dependence on agriculture of these economies means that US agricultural policy and the European Community's (EC's) Common Agricultural Policy bear heavily on the fortunes of the individual in Africa as well as throughout the developing world. The challenge now for the policy-makers of Europe and the United States is to ensure that the economic concerns of the Third World occupy a much higher priority in international policy debates and decisions than ever before. In particular, the developed world must guard against the illusion of solving their agricultural disputes at the cost of Third World producers.

This is no small challenge, but it is a challenge worthy of our times. Only comparatively recently has the world been producing enough food by volume to feed itself. The global concern about food deficit has now evaporated, but it has

Hungry Farmers

World food needs and Europe's response

This b   must be   ately
         d f   nd in

Published by Christian Aid 1989

Designed by David Walker

Printed by Stanley L Hunt (Printers) Ltd, Rushden

© Christian Aid 1989   ISBN 0 904379 13 2
PO Box 100
London
SE1 7RT

given way to a much more serious concern: to raise the purchasing power of the 700 million or so people who still do not have enough to eat properly. The twin problems of surplus production in the West and famine in the Third World are linked in the public mind, but in technical terms the link is tangential. This does not mean that the EC and the US, in particular, should not concentrate hard on the reduction or elimination of both problems.

On the question of reducing EC surpluses, the European Community has been relatively successful in the past few years, and more effective reforms are even now in the pipeline. It remains to be seen how these reforms will affect the overall situation, but it must be said that the Common Agricultural Policy (CAP) has already gone a long way towards the sort of reforms necessary for a rebalancing of world trade so that Third World production and consumption can be better stimulated.

The book is well-researched and concise, a happy combination of attributes. I recommend it unreservedly as an excellent basis for understanding the often tortuous problems of agriculture, development and food policy.

Lord Plumb, DL, MEP

Lord Plumb, Former President, European Parliament

Acknowledgements

Christian Aid's partners in Africa, Asia and Latin America provided many of the insights for this book and several people, inside and outside Christian Aid, made helpful suggestions. John Montagu made the book more readable. Valuable reactions to the first draft were received from Robert Chambers, Belinda Coote, Reginald Herbold Green, Edward Mayo, Christopher Stevens, Nick Viney and Kevin Watkins, but Christian Aid and the author are solely responsible for the final text.

A bibliography appears on page 105 but the book owes its greatest debt to three published sources: *L'Enjeu Alimentaire Nord-Sud* by Bertrand Delpeuch (with thanks also to his designer, René Schoenhenzel, for the diagrams on pages 15, 25, 29 and 79), *World Hunger – 12 Myths* by Frances Moore Lappé and Joseph Collins, and *Modernising Hunger* by Philip Raikes. *The Times* kindly gave permission for the use of the story of Noi Petsri on page 65 and the *Financial Times* for the diagram on page 39 and the quotation on page 86. Most of the projects financed by Christian Aid in Chapter 9, and the work of GK in Chapter 6, are co-financed by the Commission of the European Communities.

CHAPTER ONE

World Hunger: The Facts

Famine in Africa still haunts the conscience of the European public. The memory of the suffering, and of the generous response which followed, only a few years ago, is still fresh. Many well-known aid agencies including Christian Aid were active in this international effort to meet food shortages in Africa and elsewhere. But there were also new ones. Band Aid, Live Aid and Comic Relief were created solely to respond to the African emergency. All these funds gave more to long-term development of food production than to emergency aid. But the event which brought them into being was the Ethiopian famine of 1984-5. The immediate priority during that winter was to get food to the starving. Nightly

---

40,000 children die every day from malnutrition

---

television reports told us that hundreds were dying in refugee camps and by January 1985 it was estimated that the famine had killed 300,000.

That figure is about the same as the number of children under five who die *every week* throughout the world, most of them from hunger or diseases related to hunger.

Famine is simply hunger concentrated in time and place. What was different about Ethiopia was the ability of news reporters to capture the famine as an event, as starving people crowded into the camps. Death from hunger is not a media event but a constant, unpublicised reality. UNICEF has estimated that 40,000 children die every day (14.6 million every year) from malnutrition. In a 1986 report the World Bank said that in 1980 730 million people in the world had not received enough calories in their diet for an active working life.

An average human being, according to the UN Food and Agriculture Organisation (FAO), needs 2,400 calories per day. It is estimated that one human being in every 10 suffers from chronic hunger (receiving only about 1,500 calories per day). 40 per cent of the hungry are children under 10.

According to FAO only three in every 10 of the world's undernourished live in sub-Saharan Africa. 55 per cent of the

Chris Steele-Perkins/Magnum

The famine camps in Ethiopia brought the hungry and the news reporters

face to face.

undernourished live in Asia. But Africa has the worst levels of malnutrition and in spite of improvements in food production the numbers of hungry people there are rising faster than anywhere else.

Hunger can be measured by its effects as well as by the numbers involved. The true geography of hunger only begins to emerge if we look at the 10 countries with the highest proportion of deaths among children under five.

Under 5 deaths per 1,000 in 1987

1.	Afghanistan	304
2.	Mali	296
3.	Mozambique	295
4.	Angola	288
5.	Sierra Leone	270
6.	Malawi	267
7.	Ethiopia	261
8.	Guinea	252
9.	Burkina Faso	237
10.	Niger	232

Lower down the list come:

18.	Cambodia	208
24.	Bangladesh	191
39.	India	152
67.	Brazil	87
117.	United Kingdom	11
118.	Ireland	11

(UNICEF: *The State of the World's Children*, 1989)

Nine of the top 10 countries with the worst record of child deaths are in Africa. Yet these countries generally have much smaller populations than those in Asia, which has the greatest absolute numbers of hungry people. According to one FAO estimate, nearly half the hungry in the Third World live in India.

Thomas Malthus was an early 19th century British economist who warned that population growth tended to outstrip the increase in food supply. This is not happening today on a world scale. World food production is going up faster than population, though not in Africa, where one person in six has come to depend largely on imported grain. The well-publicised campaigns to 'feed the world' have been fairly

Most of the 70 per cent of the world's hungry who live outside Africa are hungry for reasons other than food shortage

directed at Africa's food production. But, as this book will explain, most of the 70 per cent of the world's hungry who live outside Africa are hungry for reasons other than food shortage, and their problems deserve equal attention.

"Here the problem is hunger, there's not enough food for everyone, there's not enough seed, no one has any clothes. But above all it's hunger we're worried about – as you see, children collect cassava peelings to re-peel to get the little bit of cassava left. Others collect wild mushrooms, women are pounding up cassava leaves, peelings, even mango stones. Here the land is very sandy so nothing will grow – our lands are only 20 kms away and there, the other side of the crossroads, the land is very fertile but because of the war we can't return there at the moment. Lots of children are sick now, and we're all getting very thin – we need some food."

Fatima Manuel, interviewed by Jenny Matthews in Impaca Camp, Mozambique, 1989.

Fatima Manuel, Zambezia Province, Mozambique: in need of food and peace.

9

CHAPTER TWO

World Hunger: The Causes

"The very way people think about hunger is the greatest obstacle to ending it."
(Frances Moore Lappé and Joseph Collins, 1988).

Hunger is not caused by a lack of food in the world, and it is not caused by population growth. The world produces enough grain alone to provide every human being with 1½ times the necessary calories per day – if it could be distributed equally. Over 40 per cent of the world's grain supply is now fed to animals. In 1985 India had a surplus of 24 million tonnes of wheat and rice, double the amount of food aid delivered world-wide in an average year. Yet it is in South Asia, where the seeds of the Green Revolution have led to the greatest production increases, that half the world's hungry live. In Zimbabwe, Africa's best-known surplus producer, nearly 30 per cent of all children are stunted by malnutrition. South Africa is a major exporter of maize but malnutrition there is rife, especially in the homelands.

Because population growth and hunger can occur side by side, it is often thought that the first causes the second. In fact, they have a common cause: poverty. When parents rely on children for family labour and for care in old age, and when

---

"Hunger and famine are the symptoms of poverty and under-development."
(Inter-Church Report, *The Root Causes of Hunger and Food Insufficiency in Africa*, 1985).

---

they cannot be sure that their children will survive, they need the security of larger families. In developing countries in which food supplies to poor families are known to be reliable (Cuba, China, Kerala State in India) and which have good social provision beyond the family, population growth rates have fallen. Studies show that a higher standard of living is more likely than family planning to bring down high fertility rates. The best way to reduce both population growth and hunger is to combat poverty.

Food security has been defined by the World Bank as,

"access by all people at all times to enough food for an active, healthy life". It can be considered at four levels: global, regional, country and household. We have seen that overall the world does not lack food. Often a country has a shortfall in food production and then it needs to import. The number of countries whose resources are so poor that they will never be able to grow the staple food they need is very small: in Africa, perhaps only half a dozen.

The most important level is that of the household. It is the inability of poor families to grow or buy enough food – their lack of access to land or money – which causes hunger; the rich can always buy themselves out of trouble. The European Commission recognised this in a report in 1988 which said it was, "mainly deficits in terms of household purchasing power which lead to malnutrition in Africa".

The causes of hunger can be divided into three broad groups: those concerned with food production (agro-ecological), economic causes and social/political causes.

It is obvious that hunger in the 1980s, in Africa and elsewhere, has been made worse by drought and food production problems. Much of the land available to peasant farmers is of poor quality and soil erosion has made it worse.

Mike Goldwater/Network

Relief feeding in Eritrea: where drought and war joined with poverty to produce a hungry nation.

11

Soil erosion and reduced rainfall are often the result of deforestation. Land clearance for farming, the search for fuelwood and the export of tropical woods have reduced forests at an alarming rate during this century.

"My house lies on the road from a forest area. Lumber passes along the road every day: hundreds of trucks. I look at the logs and feel like crying. Three, four, five times the Bishops' Conference of Ghana has drawn the attention of the Government to the desecration of the forest. But Ghana is poor. In my own lifetime, places I knew to be virgin forests are becoming deserts. EC nations guard their forests with religious jealousy, but continue to buy our forest products."

Mgr Peter Sarpong, Bishop of Kumasi, Ghana (February 1989).

Fifteen million hectares of forest in the Ivory Coast in 1900 had fallen to two million by 1986; in the same period Ethiopia's land under forest fell from 40 per cent to four per cent. More than 11 million hectares of forests are destroyed yearly, equalling, over three decades, an area about the size of India. Forests in Central America and Brazil have been cleared, mainly for ranching to provide beef for North American hamburger chains. The rate of reforestation in developing countries is only 10 per cent of what is necessary to meet their needs. With less vegetation to attract and hold rainwater, drought came as a final blow to lands which were already difficult for farming.

Yet developing countries, even in Africa, are still tending to grow more, not less, food each year.

Nature is not primarily to blame. Man-made famine means not only that much of the damage done to the land has been the result of human action but that men, more than women, have contributed to hunger. People who keep animals get much of the blame for overgrazing, but they are often forced on to unsuitable scrubland by farmers; especially by large-scale farmers and companies which exploit marginal land for profit. 'Land-mining' of this kind was encouraged in Sudan in the 1960s and 1970s, with the result that vulnerable lands were exhausted after five to seven years. The risk of harvest failure is increased when the best land is taken for cash crops, when wheat (which requires irrigation in many tropical zones) and maize are encouraged on land which is drought-prone, and when government farm advisers recommend

Flooded – and landless

In the Bangladesh village of Astapukur, Sonaton Soren is a sharecropper on almost four acres of land. A visit to his village just as abundant quantities of rice were being threshed by Mr Soren and his team presented an image of plenty. Then he explained that the landlord was coming tomorrow to collect his half share of the harvest. What was more, Mr Soren had to give the threshing team 3 kg of rice out of every 20 kg harvested. After harvest he will migrate to another area to work in the fields, sleeping in the open air, to support his wife and two children. It is not the floods which cause the Soren family's poverty, but the unequal distribution of land.

monocropping rather than traditional mixed farming. Although many hectares were affected by drought during the 1980s, there are also many hectares of farmland in developing countries which remain rich in resources, well-watered and productive and where the families who live nearby still go hungry.

The basic causes of hunger are economic. At the household level it is unequal access to land and lack of income, jobs and money to buy even the food that is available which keep poor people hungry. In *Poverty and Famines* (1981) Professor Amartya Sen challenged the notion that famines were the result of a falling supply of food. Famines like those in Bengal (1942-4), and in Ethiopia and the Sahel in the 1970s and

The basic causes of hunger are economic

1980s, occurred when poor families could no longer afford to buy food, or lost their 'entitlement' to it. Those who had invested their savings in animals fared no better; when famine came, cattle prices collapsed as grain prices soared. It is lack of access to food caused by poverty – what economists call lack of effective demand – which allows people to go hungry.

Governments and international agencies have tended to assess hunger by adding up the statistics of supply and demand at global, regional or national level. Enrique ter Horst from the International Fund for Agricultural Development (IFAD) warned against the statistical approach when he told the 1988 World Food Conference: "The question is on the one hand how to bring about a balanced distribution of production between regions and countries, and on the other how to stimulate an effective demand among the poor who

13

do not have access to enough food due to inadequate purchasing power."

The author Philip Raikes adds that, "certain areas and certain groups of people (the urban poor, the landless and those pushed onto marginal land) are getting steadily worse off. As the capacity to produce of poor peasants and people in marginal areas declines and becomes more insecure, so do their incomes and capacity to buy food." The aim should therefore be not to increase production in the better areas, but to increase the incomes of the poorest in the 'low-resource' areas.

World Bank figures show that the problem is one of groups of hungry people within nations rather than one of hungry nations. The re-allocation of only 5.6 per cent of India's food supply would wipe out hunger in that country. In Indonesia, which has the second largest number of hungry people, a two per cent change would do the same. Even in richer countries like the United States, the UK and Ireland there are malnourished families.

As long as people's only claim to food lies through the market, some people will die of hunger no matter how much food is produced. This was dramatically shown in Sudan in 1984-5 by the refusal of private traders to move food into remote and vulnerable areas at reasonable prices. Two years later, when Sudan had large surpluses of sorghum, the European Community paid to divert them to areas of hunger when traders were more interested in exporting them as cheap animal feed.

Until recently, farming in the Northern hemisphere was over-subsidised while farming in the South was over-taxed. Many developing countries came to independence with no other means of raising revenue than by taxing their farmers' production. In the early 1980s the price paid to producers of cocoa in Ghana represented less than half the export price; for coffee in Togo, the producer price was only one-third. The need for taxation also helps to explain the prominent role which state marketing agencies acquired in developing countries.

Most governments have also tried to meet the needs of their more vocal city populations through low consumer prices, even for the better-off, and by importing cheaper food rather than increasing opportunities for their own farmers. There are hopeful signs that this lack of price and marketing incentives for developing country farmers is being reversed.

But the economic causes of hunger go beyond the developing countries themselves. Their governments have had to make policies in an international economic and financial casino where the dice are heavily loaded against them. Northern countries have tempted them with cheap food imports, weakening already tenuous links with their own farmers. Small changes in Northern government policies can be disastrous for developing countries: the African food crisis of 1973-4 followed a three-fold increase in the world price of wheat caused by changes in US agricultural policy and a rise in Soviet cereal imports. The economies of developing countries have been rocked by the double impact of deteriorating terms of trade (falling prices of their exports) and the debt crisis. Third World debt, described more fully in Christian Aid's book *Banking on the Poor* (1988), has

Farm policies compared

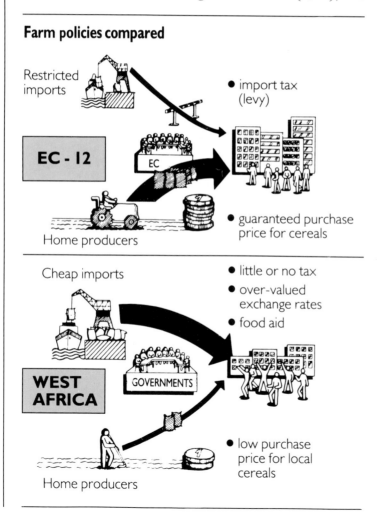

Restricted imports

- import tax (levy)

EC - 12

EC

Home producers

- guaranteed purchase price for cereals

Cheap imports

- little or no tax
- over-valued exchange rates
- food aid

WEST AFRICA

GOVERNMENTS

Home producers

- low purchase price for local cereals

Women who lost land when the Green Revolution came to India were then hired as cheap labour to work on the new crops.

pushed developing countries towards more export crop production to generate foreign exchange and into austerity programmes which have hit the poor hardest of all.

Governments have the power to change many of the social and political causes of hunger. The prime cause in several countries is conflict. The list of countries with high rates of child deaths on page 8 shows how many of these countries have been beset by war: Afghanistan, Mozambique, Angola, Ethiopia, Cambodia. Wars have the double effect of disrupting the production and distribution of food and of diverting resources to the purchase of arms. In Afghanistan and Sudan food has been consciously used as a weapon by

Women produce around 50 per cent of the world's food but own only one per cent of the world's land

warring factions. Northern governments have played a big part in the history leading up to many of these conflicts and should take more active steps towards solving them. They could begin by ending their own promotion of arms sales.

Access to food could also be improved if governments and traditional societies gave more recognition to the central role which women play in food. Women produce around 50 per cent of the world's food but own only one per cent of the world's land. In Africa two-thirds of the agricultural work is done by women. Women in developing countries can now be found doing much of the work on cash crops (working on their husbands' land), producing and preparing all the food crops and gathering fuel and water supplies, a task often taking several hours per day.

In Malawi women have to work twice as long as men on the staple maize crop, do equal amounts in the cotton fields and still find time to do all the domestic work. In India the

Famine begins at home

If history is any guide, the real causes of Third World famine may be better understood in Ireland than in Great Britain. The Irish famine of the 19th century has had deep effects on the development of Irish society in the 20th century. Much of the best agricultural land had been taken over by British settlers and planters and the original owners of the land had been retained as tenant farmers. There was little incentive to develop the land as they had no security of tenure. One of the consequences of this pattern of ownership and development of land was the famine in the 1840s.

The potato crop (the basic food of the tenant farmers) failed. Corn did grow but it had to be paid to the landlords in lieu of rent. The British Government refused to intervene, allowing free market forces to decide what would happen to the food grown in Ireland. Local Irish people were unable to pay for the corn and so food was exported from Ireland while Irish people died of starvation or emigrated in order to survive.

The more recent history of Irish farming tells another story about preserving and developing agriculture in a hostile international environment. After Independence (1922) subsistence farming continued and was combined with almost total dependence on British markets for Irish exports. From 1930 to the late 1940s the Irish government developed a policy of self-sufficiency, with the emphasis on production for the home market. Ireland joined the EC in 1973. Ireland's protective trade barriers were gradually removed, making Irish industries more vulnerable to competition from foreign products. Agriculture, however, was protected (through the Common Agricultural Policy) by support from the wealthier members of the EC. Irish farmers gained substantially, though the benefits went more to the large than to small-scale farmers.

Green Revolution increased the burden on women: many peasant families lost their land, and it was the women who were hired as low-paid seasonal labour in such tasks as transplanting, weeding and harvesting. In Honduras a women farmers' group's request for land was turned down by the authorities simply because they were women. In the Philippines a woman can acquire land only with her husband's consent. The major contribution of women to food production and preparation is often left out of official statistics, because so many tasks are performed within the household. At the end of all this work women, who are responsible for family nutrition, receive less to eat than men. In Bangladesh, one of only three countries in the world where women live shorter lives than men, they receive only

Attempts to tackle hunger with production increases often widen the gap between the hungry and the overfed

half of a man's ration. Local customs and land ownership systems stand in the way of a better deal for women as food providers.

Even government aid programmes for agriculture have rarely brought benefits to the poor and hungry. Agriculture and forestry have so far received only a small share of governmental aid and much of that has gone to large irrigation schemes to grow rice for the better-off in the towns. The European Community has put money into the expensive Diama and Manantali dams in the Senegal river valley which will revolutionise farming in this area, wiping out traditional agriculture in favour of rice-growing. Large agricultural investments of this kind aimed at increased productivity have often benefited richer farmers and have put long-term soil fertility at risk. Governments and international agencies have pinned their hopes too much on economic growth and technological improvement. Attempts to tackle hunger with production increases do not solve the basic problem of equity: they often simply widen the gap between the hungry and the overfed.

Much more can be done by developing country governments to bring about equal access to food, land and productive resources; a handful of good examples shows that this is so. But the world of food and agriculture is increasingly interdependent. Governments, banks and multinational companies in the North have a growing influence over the economies and food prospects of the South. And it is much easier for rich countries to make small changes in their policies than for poorer ones.

Why Luis and Dorcelli are hungry

Luis and Dorcelli have lived in the southernmost state of Brazil all their lives. Luis inherited a small plot of land from his father, on which they grew beans and maize for themselves and their five children. They usually had enough over to sell in the local market to cover their other needs. For the months following harvest all was well but as the year advanced they had to borrow to tide themselves over between sowing and reaping. This used not to be too much of a worry, as the government made cheap credits available to small farmers. It was they, after all, who grew most of the food for the Brazilian population.

However, when the debt crisis broke in 1982 things began to change. Commercial banks were unwilling to continue lending money to the Brazilian Government, afraid that it would not pay it back. They insisted first on an agreement between Brazil and the International Monetary Fund to 'restructure' the economy. Government expenditure was to be cut. There would be no more room for lending to peasant farmers at low interest rates. Incentives would be given instead to large farmers who were planting crops for export rather than home consumption.

Luis and Dorcelli thus had to turn to another source of finance when their money ran out at sowing time. They borrowed money from their local bank which charged them interest at the rate of 24 per cent a month. Their debt soared. Harvest came. They sold their entire crop, leaving nothing for themselves to eat but still they could not pay back the loan.

Now Luis and Dorcelli live in a small wooden shack in a poor area of the town of Sapiranga. They have no land, no stable income and are often hungry. Dorcelli and the children use the daylight hours to sew shoes at home for a pitiful wage from a local shoe factory. Luis takes odd jobs where he can. They had to sell their land to the bank to repay their loan. Now it has been taken over by a large landowner who is growing soya beans to feed European cows.

19

CHAPTER THREE

Food Mountains in Europe

"I haven't anywhere to keep all my crops. I will tear down my barns and build bigger ones, where I will store my corn and all my other goods."
(St Luke 12 vv 17-18)

The second image which caught the imagination of TV companies in the 1984-5 famine was the sight of Europe's own grain mountains. Reporters tried to locate the inter- vention stores of farm produce in their viewers' home towns and to juxtapose them with pictures of the famine. At the height of the hunger, the UK in 1984 was sitting on a record cereals crop of 26.6 million tonnes, Ireland too had a record harvest of 2.1 million tonnes, and the Common Agricultural Policy (CAP) was there to take the blame. Farmers com- plained they were being made to feel guilty for doing what they had always done – producing food – and started their

---

One of the most damaging surpluses for the Third World is sugar, but there are no visible sugar mountains

---

own 'Send-a-Tonne' campaign to help the starving. Christian Aid issued a leaflet arguing that a simple transfer of surplus food to the needy countries was not the only, nor even the best way to help them feed themselves. As Tony Jackson of Oxfam put it: "Simply exporting our surplus problem and calling it food aid is no solution."

The food mountains have subsided and no longer make the headlines they once did. What has happened to them over the past five years?

EC rules enable farmers to sell some of their products into state intervention stores at guaranteed prices rather than face a loss in selling them cheaply on the open market. This avoids a glut and helps to keep up the prices paid to farmers. The main products stored in this way are cereals, butter, milk powder, beef and veal, wine, olive oil, tobacco and now oilseeds.

Not all products supported by the CAP go into intervention

stores. One of the most damaging surpluses for the Third World is sugar, but there are no visible sugar mountains; the EC has other ways of dealing with that surplus (See Box, page 34). The EC also withdraws surplus perishable foods (fruit and vegetables) from the market and destroys them. Apples, pears, peaches, mandarins, oranges, lemons, table grapes, apricots, tomatoes, cauliflowers and aubergines are destroyed every year in this way.

The intervention system is managed in the UK by the Intervention Board for Agricultural Produce (in Ireland by the Department of Agriculture), which rents most of the silos and cold stores it needs from farmers or commercial companies. The Intervention Board does the initial buying and is then reimbursed by the EC for storage and for any loss incurred when it resells the products at a lower price. Whether stored food is of any use as food aid depends on quality and price. A large proportion of the cereals stored is intended as feed grain for animals and is not checked against standards for human consumption. There are generally cheaper surpluses available on the open market than in intervention stores, and governments shopping around for food aid pay the lower prices outside the stores.

During the 'famine year' (September 1984 to September 1985) cereals in store in the EC almost trebled, from six million to nearly 17 million tonnes. Other stored surpluses continued to rise over the following year, leading *The Times* in November 1986 to call the CAP "a monster which threatens to engulf Europe in disputes and to disrupt the agriculture of the whole world". The huge cost of storage had by then overtaken the shame of 'hunger amid plenty' as the chief target of criticism. In the space of two years, the amounts stored in the four main mountains of cereals, milk powder, butter and beef moved like this:

	November 1986	December 1988
	Tonnes	*Tonnes*
Cereals	16,780,000	10,752,000
Skimmed milk powder	1,100,000	14,000
Butter	1,500,000	146,000
Beef and veal	620,000	723,000

Has the CAP at last been brought under control? Its most costly sector has been milk products. There was a particular effort to reduce dairy surpluses, first through quotas introduced in 1984 and tightened in 1986, and then through a

21

scheme in 1987 to dispose cheaply of old stocks of butter (See Box, page 24). The plans have worked but one result has been a growth in the beef surplus as European farmers have moved out of dairying and have had to slaughter five million cattle. Some have moved into sheep farming and others have increased their cereal production. In the case of cereals CAP managers cannot take the same credit. The 1988 drought which hit the world's largest cereals producers in North America made it much easier for the EC to sell off its grain surpluses on world markets, for example to the USSR, which still imports more grain than all the low-income developing countries together.

The effect of the American drought on world food stocks raised a question which two years earlier seemed barely relevant. Is the world running out of grain? The Sahelian and Ethiopian famines of 1973-4 (unlike those of 1984-5) took place during a world grain shortage, but then production increased in the late 1970s and early 1980s, especially among importers like India and China which moved closer to self-sufficiency. Now, once again, for the past two years the world has consumed more grain than it has produced.

Grain stocks, production and consumption

Total in store (worldwide) millions of tonnes

	ALL GRAINS	WHEAT
End of 1987–8 marketing year	400.8	146.3
1988–9 (estimate)	301.0	116.5
1989–90 (provisional)	288.2	111.8

Production and consumption (worldwide) millions of tonnes

	ALL GRAINS		WHEAT	
	Production	Consumption	Production	Consumption
1987–8	1606.4	1664.9	501.8	531.6
1988–9	1552.8	1652.6	500.2	530.0
1989–90	1671.0	1683.7	533.4	538.1

Source: US Dept of Agriculture

Global cereal stocks in the summer of 1989 were at their lowest levels, in relation to world demand, for 40 years. The 'safe' level of these reserves, according to FAO, is 17 per cent of consumption, and they had fallen to this figure by 1989. A ratio of 17 per cent at EC level means that the Community should keep a stock of 20 million tonnes, higher than the grain mountain at its mid-1980s peak, but a committee of the European Parliament in 1987 was content to accept a surplus of 12-15 million tonnes as normal.

Building the mountain: Europe's mechanised harvesting helps the cereal stocks to grow.

With over 40 per cent of the world's grain fed to animals, global figures are an unreliable guide to the prospects for world hunger. What matters is where the stocks are, and who has the money to buy them. Out of total world cereal stocks of 282 million tonnes in 1984, 158 million were stored in developed countries, 108 million in Asia and only 6½ million in Africa. This imbalance is also reflected in the International Wheat Council's forecasts for grain production and consumption in the year 2000. The Council believes that to meet rising demand developing countries will have both to produce more and to import more, taking an estimated two thirds of the world's cereal imports by 2000. However, that will depend on how much encouragement small farmers receive to increase their production of local staple foods. Their degree of success will decide the extent of rural hunger in developing countries in the 21st century.

Food surpluses and hunger are two separate problems. The size of food mountains in the EC is not in itself a problem for the Third World, but some of the ways suggested for disposing of those stocks are. Attempts to get rid of unwanted

23

European farm surpluses through subsidised export pro-grammes, or through food aid, can threaten the livelihoods of Third World farmers if this food reaches the market at a lower price than that of local produce. The European Parliament committee which examined the stocks problem in 1987 made a range of suggestions, less harmful to the Third World, for disposing of stocks and preventing them building up again:

— disposal to special groups of consumers, eg butter and beef for pensioners.
— increased use in confectionery and ice cream.

The Dairy Box

Until 1988 dairy products were the CAP's most expensive regime, though not the one with the greatest effects on the Third World. The EC is the world's leading exporter of dairy products, with 60 per cent of world trade in butter in 1987. Dairy products account for almost one-fifth in value of all EC farm production and nearly half the value of EC food aid. Aid in milk powder and butteroil to large dairy development programmes in India (Operation Flood) and China takes a considerable share of the EC food aid budget. But dairy exports go mainly to Middle Eastern and middle-income countries (such as Saudi Arabia, Algeria and Iran) rather than low-income developing countries.

Minimum world prices are set by the International Dairy Arrangement, part of the General Agreement on Tariffs and Trade (GATT). As the USSR is not yet a member of GATT, it has been able to benefit from cheap sales of surplus EC butter, the '7 pence per pound' sales, while the EC has had to charge the agreed minimum prices to other countries which are members of GATT.

Since 1986 over-production in milk has been cut more successfully than in any other CAP product, through the use of quotas. Milk quotas were first agreed for each member state and each individual farmer in 1984. High levies have to be paid by any farmer who exceeds his quota of deliveries to the dairy. The quotas were initially set too high, at 120 per cent of demand, but a quota cut of 9.5 per cent was agreed at the end of 1986, which has stopped further surpluses building up. In addition, because of the high cost of supporting dairy farmers, member states agreed in 1987 to lend the EC an extra £2.2 billion to get rid of existing butter stocks through cheap exports and increased use in animal feed.

EC milk production fell from 109.5 million tonnes in 1984 to 98.5 million in 1988. In the UK, dairy farmers' average incomes rose by 25 per cent (in Ireland by more than 17 per cent) in 1988, despite a general fall in farm incomes. But many smaller farmers have been driven out of dairying, in part because quotas froze the existing inequalities between large and small producers. Some European farmers' groups have suggested the 'quantum' system, which offers a fixed price up to a certain volume of production per worker, as a fairer way of applying quotas.

— more incorporation into animal feeds and 'on-farm' use.
— alternative industrial uses: starch, sweeteners and bio-ethanol as a motor fuel can be manufactured from maize, but research and production costs can be prohibitive.
— alternative crops: switching to legumes (beans and peas) and high-protein animal feeds which are not in surplus.
— alternative uses of land, eg conservation and tourism.
— destruction: despite the likely reaction from public opinion and the media, this might be the only answer for surplus wine and old stocks of butter and tobacco.

The two main reasons for Europe's large food stocks are price support and technological advance. Government subsidies in the EC to beef and dairy production average US$400 per cow per year, more than the average income of a Third World farmer, while the subsidy per cow in the United

The Quota and Quantum Principles in Dairy Production

For 3 farms   A   B   C

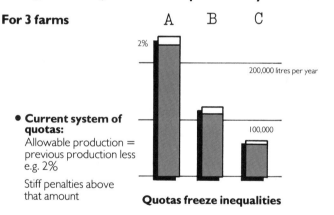

• **Current system of quotas:**
Allowable production = previous production less e.g. 2%

Stiff penalties above that amount

Quotas freeze inequalities

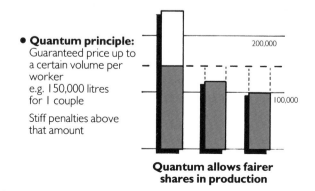

• **Quantum principle:**
Guaranteed price up to a certain volume per worker
e.g. 150,000 litres for 1 couple

Stiff penalties above that amount

Quantum allows fairer shares in production

States is a staggering US$835. Increased use of fertilisers, machinery and compound feeds and the development of factory farming have brought dramatic increases in yields in the EC in recent years. The average yield for wheat went up by nearly 50 per cent between 1973 and 1985 and the amount of milk produced by each dairy cow rose by 21 per cent between 1974 and 1985.

The reasons for the food mountains are now widely accepted, and the brakes have to some extent been applied. Alternatives are at least being explored. But, as we shall see, it is the protection of agriculture in the developing countries which should now be of paramount concern.

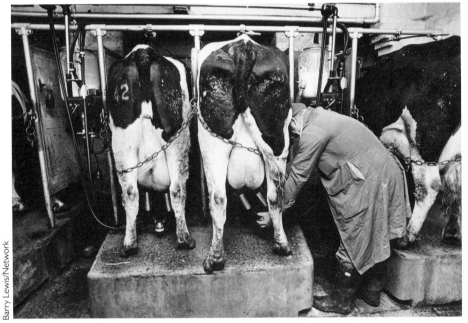

Production penned in: every drop of milk these British cows produce is now subject to marketing quotas.

CHAPTER FOUR

The Common Agricultural Policy

"Woe to those who add house to house and join field to field until everywhere belongs to them and they are the sole inhabitants of the land."
(Isaiah 5 v 8)

It was in the late 1950s, with memories of post-war food shortages in Europe still fresh in their minds, that politicians of the original six European Community (EC) countries invented the CAP. Its objectives, set out in Article 39 of the Treaty of Rome, are to:
– increase productivity by promoting technical progress and the best use of labour.
– ensure a fair standard of living for the farm community.
– stabilise markets.
– ensure food supplies.
– ensure reasonable consumer prices.
    When the CAP was put in place in 1962, it was based on three principles: a single market for farm products, pre-

"To increase agricultural productivity by promoting technical progress and by ensuring the rational development of agricultural production and the optimum utilisation of the factors of production, in particular labour."
(Treaty of Rome, Article 39).

ference for EC farmers over those outside, and joint financing by the member states. Farm production is supported by three main mechanisms: guaranteed minimum prices; protection against imports by levies and other import controls such as duties, tariffs and quotas; and export subsidies to assist cheap sales of surpluses on the world market. Other subsidies encourage the internal use of products in surplus. There is also a fund (the Guidance Fund) to encourage structural changes on farms, which has never taken more than five per cent of the CAP budget. The rest has always been swallowed up by the costs of price support, storage and disposal (the Guarantee Fund). In 1987 16 per cent of CAP funds was spent on storage and 40 per cent on export subsidies. In that year the cost of the CAP was £17.5 billion, two-thirds of the entire EC budget. At the European Summit of February 1988, maximum CAP spending was fixed at just under £18 billion and it was agreed to stop it rising faster than the EC's Gross National Product.

Consumers do not have cheap food, nor have farm jobs been preserved

The diagram opposite shows how the price system works. Every year the EC Farm Ministers, after long hours of bargaining, set a target price for most products, indicating what producers should receive. A little lower comes the threshold price, the minimum price at which imports are allowed to enter; variable levies span the difference between the threshold price and the world price to prevent imports coming in more cheaply. Below that is the intervention price, the floor price at which national governments are obliged to buy in surpluses. Member states meet regularly to fix the level of export subsidies to be paid to traders to take account of the difference between Community prices and the lower world price. The intervention system used to be an open-ended guarantee to buy up any amount of surpluses but recent EC attempts to cut costs have begun to restore intervention buying to its original role as a 'safety net'. There are now limits on the periods when intervention stores are open, on quality standards and, for some products such as cereals, on the total amount of produce eligible for support (known as 'stabilisers').

How far has the CAP achieved its aims and who has reaped the benefits? Productivity increases have been achieved but consumers do not have cheap food, nor have farm jobs been preserved. From 1973 to 1985 farm production in the EC increased by 1.8 per cent per year, while demand for food was rising by only half a per cent. The price support system and technological change have pushed productivity so far that self-sufficiency (not mentioned in the Treaty of Rome) has overtaken security of supply as the ideal and many products have gone into surplus. This is true even where it would make better economic sense to continue to import; the EC oilseed sector is not yet self-sufficient but it has received high subsidies. It costs almost five times more to

How the CAP supports the price of wheat

Paid into EAGGF*

Paid by EAGGF*

Target price

Threshold price

Intervention price

Variable import levy

Export subsidy (variable)

World market price

(variable)

World market price

(variable)

EC as an importer

EC as an exporter

*EAGGF: European Agricultural Guarantee and Guidance Fund

produce a tonne of rapeseed oil in the EC than to purchase a tonne of palm oil from such countries as Indonesia. The growth in self-sufficiency rates in the EC is shown in the table

29

(where 100 per cent is self-sufficiency and anything higher is a surplus):

	1973-4	1985-6
Total cereals (excl. rice)	90	114
Common wheat	106	121
White sugar	91	137
Beef and veal	100	106
Skimmed milk powder	164	133
Butter	110	132

Consumers in the EC pay extra for their food not only through taxes which finance the CAP but through higher prices in the shops caused by the minimum farm prices set by the EC. EC countries also give national aid to agriculture. The National Consumer Council (NCC) estimates that during the 1980s farm produce has been 70 per cent more expensive on the Community market than on the world market. Balancing all the gains and losses, the NCC claims that there is a gap of nearly £20 billion between the total paid out by consumers and tax-payers and the total support directed at farmers. In other words, every £65 that the farm community gains costs consumers and tax-payers over £100. Much of the CAP support, in fact, goes to storage, trading and agribusiness interests; according to one estimate £6 billion per year (a quarter of the EC budget) goes to traders alone. Farming, as we normally picture it, is now only one link in a food chain comprising big business corporations.

These consumer costs might be more acceptable if the CAP had kept most of the EC's farmers on the land. But it has failed. Not only have average farm incomes remained static but the

Jobs in farming in the EC have been cut to 40 per cent of their number in 1960

gap between rich and poor has widened. This is inevitable with a guaranteed price policy which means that the more a farmer produces the more he earns: the largest farms get the greatest benefits. The average number of farm workers per 100 hectares in the EC is 15; but in the UK the figure is 4 and in Greece 52. Jobs in farming in the EC have been cut to 40 per cent of their number in 1960. Between 1960 and 1985 the EC lost 1,300 farm jobs per day. The loss of farm income and jobs is not yet as serious as in the USA, but it is evidence of a great concentration of EC farmland among the richer producers: the process which Isaiah condemned at the start of the chapter.

Studies have estimated that the largest 25 per cent of EC farms receive 75 per cent of CAP support and account for 73 per cent of total output. It is striking that the world's greatest surplus producer, the USA, now has a mere three per cent of its workforce on the land, while the EC has eight per cent (UK only two per cent and Ireland 14 per cent), and the world's greatest grain importer, the USSR, has 19 per cent. We should consider what these 'production successes' mean in terms of concentration of wealth, exodus from the land and the disappearance of small family farmers. A continent like Africa, with 65 per cent of its workforce on the land and so few alternative jobs, simply cannot afford to copy the farming pattern of the North. Similarly, we cannot contemplate CAP reform in terms of eliminating 'small uneconomic farms' without thinking of what this means for the farmers themselves.

"I have always thought it sad and crazy that the CAP, which set out to preserve jobs in the countryside, then proceeded to give huge grants to farmers who put up modern buildings filled with labour-saving equipment. Not only did this grant scheme get rid of many jobs on farms; it also favoured the better-educated farmer who could tackle the awesome paperwork."
(Nick Viney, sheep and dairy farmer, Dorset)

Who really pays the cost of the surpluses? Consumers are only half of the answer: the Third World is the other half. This is because the EC has chosen not to keep its surpluses to itself but to dispose of them cheaply on world markets. The CAP's effects on developing countries vary according to the country and the product. There are large-scale exporters like Argentina which try to compete with the subsidised exports of the industrialised countries. There are smaller exporters like the sugar cane producing countries, highly vulnerable to world market changes. There are also small producers of food for domestic or regional markets which face competition from cheap imported food. But in general the disposal of European surpluses, either as subsidised exports or as food aid, is harmful to farming in the Third World. It may offer

The Cereal Story

Around the world 200 million tonnes of cereals were traded in 1987-8: 104 million tonnes of wheat, 83 million tonnes of coarse grains (mainly maize) and 11 million tonnes of rice. Almost 90 per cent of the world wheat trade is in the hands of five big companies: Cargill, Continental, Louis Dreyfus, Bunge y Born and Andre.

Major exporters of wheat (1986–7) as a percentage of world trade

Major importers of wheat (1986–7)

In the mid-1970s the EC still received 10 per cent of the world's cereal imports, but now it is the third biggest exporter of wheat. Between 1973 and 1983 Africa's cereal imports increased three-fold; while imports of wheat and rice have risen sharply, the production of local cereals like maize, sorghum and millet has been undermined. By 1985 developing countries were taking 55 per cent of world grain imports.

At the end of the 1980s, following the North American drought, world cereal stocks had fallen and prices had risen. But there is little danger of the world's starving purely for lack of cereal stocks. In 1987-8 13 million tonnes of cereal food aid were shipped (five per cent of developed country stocks),

while the world continues to feed more than 600 million tonnes of cereals per year to livestock, including 62 per cent of all cereals grown in the EC. The trend is still towards increased yields and production, with consumption static in developed countries.

Through the 1980s the EC struggled to bring cereal production and its cost under control. It tried to set a 'guarantee threshold' – a limit on total production which would trigger a cut in the price paid to producers once it was exceeded. But farm ministers, especially in Germany where the votes of small cereal growers can make or break coalition governments, were reluctant to agree to price cuts. In 1986 a co-responsibility levy was introduced, making farmers pay three per cent of their selling price towards the cost of disposal of their cereals.

In 1988 EC member states set their seal on the 'stabiliser' system: a production limit of 160 million tonnes of cereals was adopted for the whole of the Community. If this is exceeded, there is an automatic price cut of three per cent in the following year and all but the smallest farmers pay an extra three per cent co-responsibility levy. This system is weaker than the individual quotas introduced for dairy farmers and, with yields still rising, is unlikely to cut production. The 'green money' method of adopting different exchange rates for farm prices can also protect farmers from nominal price cuts: in April 1989 British cereal farmers gained 4 per cent from the improved rate of the 'green pound'. If the stabiliser system fails to curb overall production, it may have little effect on the bigger farmers and squeeze out more of the smaller ones.

some short-term balance of payments relief to food-importing countries but it threatens longer-term agricultural development. The CAP damages Third World farming in seven ways:

● The dumping of surpluses like cereals can compete with local food production.

● The dumping of surpluses like sugar and beef can reduce export prices and opportunities for products which some developing countries export.

● The CAP puts up trade barriers against products which developing countries would like to export to the EC but

EC tariff barriers close off possible markets for Third World farmers

which compete with the CAP, such as fruit, vegetables and processed farm products.

● By protecting European farmers from the ups and downs of world prices, the CAP passes price instability on to developing country farmers.

● By importing animal feeds from developing countries, the CAP helps to encourage export crop production there, sometimes at the expense of food crops.

● European food products reinforce dependence on foods which developing countries may not easily be able to produce themselves (especially wheat).

● The cost of the CAP swamps the Community budget, leaving less money for development aid and for restructuring farming in the EC.

Even where the EC does not dump surpluses but aims only for self-sufficiency, as in oilseeds, its tariff barriers close off possible markets for Third World farmers. These tariffs rise the more a developing country tries to add value to its farm products by processing them before they are sent to Europe. For example, the tariffs on soya products from Asia and Latin America are for raw soya beans nil, soymeal seven per cent, crude oil 10 per cent, refined oil 15 per cent and margarine 25 per cent. Fresh pineapples attract a duty of nine per cent, canned pineapples 32 per cent and pineapple juice 42 per cent. For the poorest countries trying to develop their agricultural trade, the CAP can be a mighty obstacle.

During the 1980s the CAP has come under great pressure for reform. But, within the range of interests involved, the voices of developing countries have been among the weakest. Small producers and farm workers in the Third

World are heard even less than their governments. European farmers' lobbies and agribusiness have been traditionally the most powerful in shaping the CAP. Other groups, such as environmental and consumer groups, have gained influence in recent years. The two greatest pressures for reform have

Spooning It Out

The EC produces one-third more sugar than it needs but there are no visible sugar mountains. The way in which the EC disposes of its surpluses is to dump between three and four million tonnes each year on the world market. This helps to drive prices down (according to estimates, by 10-15 per cent) and to reduce the value of the exports produced by millions of poor sugar cane workers in the Third World. From being a net importer of sugar in 1973, the EC boosted its production of sugar beet until it accounted for 22 per cent of world free market exports in 1985. The EC is now the world's biggest sugar producer.

The surge in European beet sugar is due to high guaranteed prices which the CAP offers on its sugar quotas. Every five years a production quota is set for each EC country. Guaranteed prices are paid on the 'A' quota, meant to represent the amount of sugar the EC needs, and on the 'B' quota, fixed to cover unexpected shortfalls. Farmers and processors are also allowed to produce 'C' sugar which receives no price support but which can be exported cheaply. The sugar support system is said to be self-financing, paid for almost entirely by the co-responsibility levies on the farmers. But the farmers receive such a good price for their sugar that the cost is really met not only by the consumer, through higher prices in the shops, but by Third World sugar producers, through the dumping of cheap surpluses. It is the

classic case of a CAP support system where the consumer and the Third World lose and where there is no incentive for the EC to reform it because there is little cost to the Community budget.

There are two reasons why sugar quotas have encouraged over-production while milk quotas have succeeded in cutting it. Sugar quotas were set too high. They now stand at more than two million tonnes above what the EC needs. Secondly, the sugar quota simply sets a limit on production up to which subsidies are paid; it does not penalise extra production, in the way that the milk quota system does. Guaranteed prices and export subsidies are so high on 'A' and 'B' sugar that producers can afford to sell 'C' sugar on the world market without subsidy.

While the EC was increasing its share of the world market, it was also refusing to take part in the International Sugar Agreement which tried to fix a minimum world price for sugar. The EC's one saving grace for traditional cane exporters has been the Sugar Protocol under which 17 former colonies (16 in Africa, the Caribbean and the Pacific, plus India) enjoy quotas of sugar exports to the EC at the higher prices paid to beet farmers in Europe. The countries to benefit most from this annual 1.4 million tonne quota are Mauritius (with 38 per cent of the total), Fiji, Guyana, Jamaica and Swaziland. The Sugar Protocol is a lifeline to several countries which depend on good prices

come from spiralling costs and from competition with the USA in world trade.

Among the main reform proposals, *price cutting* – that is, reducing farm subsidies – is the policy now most favoured in the UK to bring costs and surpluses down. But other countries

This European beet sugar will soon be on its way to compete in price with Third World sugar cane.

for their sugar exports because they do not have the natural conditions suitable for other crops. But it does not help countries like Brazil and the Philippines which have to rely on the world market price.

From the Third World's point of view, the CAP sugar regime is the one most in need of reform – and the least likely to see it. To raise the world price and increase export outlets for the poorest sugar cane producers, the EC could adjust its production quotas to the level of its own consumption needs (less the 1.4 million tonnes imported from traditional suppliers), getting rid of the surpluses dumped on the world market, as has happened in the dairy sector. It could support a new International Sugar Agreement to set a minimum world price. It should maintain the Sugar Protocol, on the basis that cane growers have fewer options for diversifying into other crops than European beet farmers. At the same time, it should offer help to cane producers to switch, wherever possible, to other products, especially food crops like those grown by former sugar workers in the Philippines.

in the EC have a greater proportion of small family farmers than the UK and realise what price cuts would mean for them: more farm jobs lost. It is also debatable whether they would in the short-term reduce over-production. Farming has a high proportion of fixed costs (land, buildings, equipment), so that reduction in unit prices may at first lead farmers to compensate by increasing production in order to cover these costs. Price cuts would have to be severe before they checked the production of the bigger farmers; in the meantime more smaller farmers would be bankrupt.

Co-responsibility, already introduced for cereals, sugar and milk, is a production tax paid by farmers to help pay for the disposal of surpluses. *Quotas* and *quantum subsidies* are the 'opposite' to price cuts, because they limit the amount of production eligible for support but often guarantee high prices within those limits. Quotas now operate in milk, where they have been quite effective (see Dairy Box on page 24) and sugar where they have not. The quantum system is fairer to the smaller farmer because it guarantees a minimum level of production per worker and reduces support to the bigger farms.

Direct income aids and other compensation payments like early retirement are seen as further ways of discouraging high levels of production. A limited scheme for direct aids was agreed by the EC early in 1989. A year earlier another small scheme was approved for *'setaside'*, paying farmers to let land lie fallow, always with the risk that they will produce more intensively on their remaining land. *Deficiency payments* are a system, once used in the UK, which guarantees

---

Some reform proposals merely help to dispose of surpluses and do nothing to reduce them

---

prices for farmers but does not pass the costs on to consumers. *Intervention buying* has already been reduced, especially in cereals, and there are minor attempts to *diversify crop uses and production* especially towards forestry. *Controls on the use of nitrogen* fertilisers, through quotas or taxes, would cut production by reducing yields and restore a less intensive form of cultivation, more friendly to the environment.

Some of these reform proposals would reduce over-production; others would maintain production levels by transferring surpluses to world markets. Reducing over-production reduces the competition which the CAP creates for developing countries, but measures like co-responsibility levies merely help to dispose of surpluses and do nothing to reduce them. They make the CAP easier and less costly to manage in Europe, but they are the worst solution for developing countries because they assume that there are always markets onto which surpluses can be dumped.

The evidence of recent policies is that the most effective measure for reducing surpluses has been milk quotas. When quotas are suggested for other products, policy-makers often plead 'administrative difficulties', but it is hard to believe that these could not be overcome. Cereals have recently become subject to the much weaker 'stabiliser' controls (see Box,

---

The cost of drastic price cuts would be fewer farmers and even more concentration of wealth and land

---

page 32). Even if the alternative policy of drastic price cuts worked, the cost would be fewer farmers and even more concentration of wealth and land. Apart from the question of economic and social justice in Europe, this would be quite the wrong signal to send to farming in the Third World.

Critics like the German MEP Katharina Focke have long called for greater coherence between EC aid policy and its other policies like agriculture and trade. EC aid policy supports food security in developing countries as well as crop diversification. But the disposal of European surpluses threatens food security, and tariffs against processed farm products have joined forces with falling commodity prices and Third World debt to prevent diversification. Frau Focke has called for developing countries to be given greater weight in the CAP debate through the setting up of permanent machinery in the European Commission to examine the effects on the Third World of changes in the CAP. This call for 'impact analysis' has been supported by several European voluntary agencies who also argue that the EC should make good any damage done to Third World interests when the CAP is changed. But the EC has now made clear that further moves towards cutting over-production will have to be agreed with other major producer countries in the GATT talks on farm trade. In the language of agricultural trade wars, the EC has opted for multilateral, not unilateral disarmament.

CHAPTER FIVE

World Agricultural Trade

"Food imports are not just a foreign exchange problem: they also make a country lose touch with its sense of its own history and geography. The mass consumption of wheat, which comes from another geographical area, ended the usefulness of the Andes. Peruvians, without moving from their land, are exiled from their own history."
(Alan Garcia Perez, President of Peru, 1986).

The European Community is the largest importer and the second largest exporter of farm products in the world. In 1987 it had agricultural imports of £34 billion and exports of £19 billion. Half of its imports come from the Third World and these represent one-third of the Third World's exports. Just under half the EC's farm exports go to Third World countries and these make up 30 per cent of their agricultural imports. The five leading products imported from the Third World are coffee; tropical fruits, vegetables and nuts; animal feeds; woods; and cocoa. The five biggest sources of supply to the EC are Brazil (a runaway leader), Ivory Coast, Argentina, Thailand and China. The EC's main exports to the

---

Many industrialised countries are responsible for export dumping and lowering world prices

---

Third World are cereals, dairy products, beef and sugar. It is the world's largest dairy exporter, the largest free market exporter of sugar, second in beef and second in cereals. Its most important markets for dairy products and beef are in the Middle East and North Africa; only in the Middle East and Africa is the EC ahead of the United States as a food exporter.

Despite some barriers to trade with the Third World as a whole, the EC has granted preferential import arrangements to African, Caribbean and Pacific countries (ACP) in sugar, beef and bananas and to ACP, North African and Middle Eastern countries for fruit and vegetables. The Third World sends more food to the EC than it receives from the Community.

Industrialised countries as a whole, however, have gradually replaced developing countries as the major agricultural exporters, and since the early 1970s they have become net food exporters. More recently, developing countries have become net importers. Meanwhile since 1960 world farm trade has been growing twice as fast as farm production. The last 30 years have seen rich countries stepping up their farm exports on world markets in a growing trade and subsidy war which has saturated the market and forced prices down.

Many industrialised countries are responsible for export dumping and lowering world prices. The EC, with its high internal price policy, and the United States, which has encouraged its largest farm corporations to over-produce and dump at low prices, have caused chaos on world markets. The US Export Enhancement Programme began to undercut EC exports in 1984 with wheat sales to Egypt, a traditional

Developing countries' food trade balance turns negative

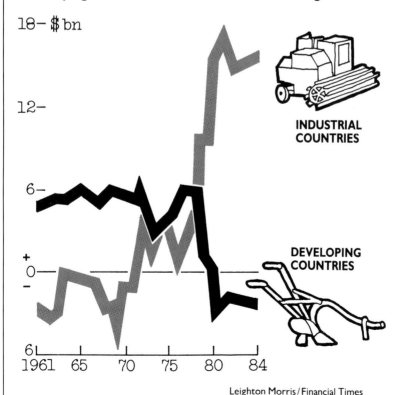

Leighton Morris / Financial Times

Christian Aid/Maggie Murray

A market in Bamako, the capital of Mali: will exporters in Europe and the USA allow Mali's farmers to feed her cities?

French market, and in 1985-6 provoked greater suffering in Thailand (the main rice exporter) by forcing a 35 per cent cut in the world price of rice. Two hectares of farmland in every five in the USA now produce food for export.

All developed countries subsidise their farm production, except Australia and New Zealand which have exceptional natural advantages. The subsidies from consumers and tax-payers to farming in developed countries amount to well over 200 billion dollars per year. Japanese farmers receive three times the world price for their rice and produce so much that some has to be sold as animal feed at half the world price. Between 1980 and 1986 farm subsidies increased from 15 to 35 per cent of farmers' incomes in the USA, from 36 to 49 per cent of incomes in the EC and from 54 to 75 per cent in Japan. Little wonder that farmers in Mali, a country on the edge of self-sufficiency, or in Argentina which has natural advantages for grain and meat but cannot afford to subsidise, should feel victims of unfair competition. Argentina, the world's fourth largest debtor, lost over two billion dollars in farm export earnings in 1984 as a result of low world prices caused by trade protection.

In this climate of farm trade friction, especially across the Atlantic, the 96 nations who make up GATT (the General Agreement on Tariffs and Trade) met in Punta del Este, Uruguay, in 1986 to launch a new round of international trade talks (the Uruguay Round). Since its creation in 1948 GATT had largely left agriculture out of its regulation of trade

The agriculture talks are dominated by the industrialised exporters

in goods: countries were permitted to limit imports of farm products and to subsidise their exports. It was agreed that the Uruguay Round would try to bring order to the farm trade chaos. In the negotiations so far, agriculture has proved to be the most contentious subject of the 15 under discussion. The agriculture talks are dominated by the industrialised exporters, worried about their budgets and trade relations, with little attention paid to the principal victims, the producers and consumers of developing countries.

All are agreed on the need to cut over-production but there is little agreement on how to do it. A brief survey of the main negotiating positions, with some comparisons of ways in which governments support their agriculture, will show the gap which has to be bridged.

The USA offers farmers a voluntary package of benefits to support prices and farm incomes provided they agree to take some of their land out of production ('setaside'). The benefits involve the government in setting a target price and a (lower) loan rate, at which a farmer can loan or sell his crop to a government credit corporation. The government then offers the farmer a 'deficiency payment' to make up the difference between the loan rate and the target price, but it is the loan rate which sets the price on the US and, to a large extent, the world market. In recent years the government has been cutting the target price and the loan rate to save costs but increasing its export subsidies to meet competition on world markets. Farms in the USA are bigger than those in the EC and, if subsidies were reduced or abolished, American agriculture would be more competitive than European. The USA has therefore called for the world-wide elimination of all direct and indirect subsidies (including export subsidies) and import barriers within 10 years: in other words, a return to the free market.

The EC has proposed a more cautious approach. This

would start with an emergency programme to set minimum prices and share markets in the most troubled sectors of cereals, sugar and dairy products, and would lead on to a gradual reduction of domestic and export subsidies – though not their elimination. The EC would also like to place new import restrictions on cereal substitutes (see Box on animal feeds, page 70), which GATT currently forbids. The EC would generally rely on market management rather than market forces.

The US objective of liberalising farm trade, however, is shared by the Cairns Group, 13 nations who have in common only an ability to sell their farm products competitively in the world without export subsidies (Argentina, Australia, Brazil, Canada, Chile, Colombia, Hungary, Indonesia, Malaysia, New Zealand, Philippines, Thailand and Uruguay). State support to farmers is much smaller in the Cairns Group countries. Australia operates loan guarantee schemes to stabilise farmers' earnings, largely with funds from the farmers themselves; only rarely is government money used. Argentina fixes domestic prices for cereals, so that farmers receive some subsidy from consumers, but these prices are still below the export price on world markets. Seeking common ground between the US and EC positions, these self-styled 'fair-traders' call for an immediate freeze on internal subsidies and also want to see an end to export subsidies and import barriers after 10 years.

Japan has one of the highest levels of protection for its farming, arguing that agriculture has functions which are social as well as economic. It escapes much of the flak directed at EC protection because it is not a major dumper of surpluses. Japan would be happy to see export subsidies phased out but wants to retain domestic support for its farmers as well as import controls.

Developing countries are largely net importers of food products and carry little weight in GATT, but a lead in presenting their views has been taken by Jamaica. Jamaica urges support for efforts by developing countries to expand their food production to self-sufficiency level and wants to see food aid maintained, financial aid increased and commodity prices stabilised.

Farmers benefit from higher world prices but consumers need compensation for dearer food

The positions of Jamaica and Argentina show that any fluctuations in world food prices caused by export dumping and new trade agreements affect food-importing and food-exporting countries, and groups within those countries, differently. Farmers benefit from higher world prices but consumers need compensation for dearer food. World food prices can have a dramatic effect on a country's balance of payments. Almost half the export earnings of the least developed countries now pays for the food they import and a growing proportion goes to pay off their debt. Developing country debt had exceeded 1,200 billion dollars by 1989, recalling former President Nyerere of Tanzania's famous question: "Should we continue to try to pay on the terms set, even at the cost of letting our people starve?" Middle-income countries may have even more problems with their food import bills. Food imports to North Africa and the Middle East rose by a massive 15 per cent per annum from 1972 to 1982, with Egypt alone importing an annual seven million tonnes of cereals.

Compensation for the poorest consumers in food-importing countries, therefore, needs to be planned by the member nations of GATT from the outset: increased aid to agriculture, food aid and improved access for tropical and

Developing countries need to increase regional self-sufficiency in locally produced staple food

processed farm products need to be carefully considered. But for developing country farmers (the majority of their populations) and for food-exporting countries, higher world prices would be a blessing.

Reliance on food imports is a viable option for developing countries only if they have steady economic growth and are creating alternative jobs to food farming. This is not the case for most developing countries, which need to increase regional self-sufficiency in locally produced staple food. To achieve this, they will often need to protect their farmers against cheap imports, for example by taxing imported food. The US and Cairns Group proposals to phase out all farm import controls might imperil the right of developing countries to protect their domestic agriculture and could subject the world's most vulnerable farmers to free market competition.

Food produced, even at a somewhat higher cost, by small producers under sustainable conditions is increasingly

A Tale of Two Farmers in Zimbabwe

Joyce Tazvitya farms in a 'communal area'. Before Independence, black people were restricted to farming these areas which are crowded, have low rainfall and poor soil. There is severe overgrazing and Joyce's family is very poor. Their crops yield barely enough to feed the family, let alone provide the surplus needed to buy clothes and pay school fees. There is plenty of food in the shops but how can they afford it?

Before Independence, Mrs Charenzve and her family were also forced to farm in overcrowded and infertile 'Tribal Trust Lands', the old name for communal areas. Their harvest in those days was 5-7 bags of millet, not enough to feed them for a year. Thanks to a government resettlement scheme the family now has a small portion of what used to be a commercial farm. The result is spectacular. Last year Mrs Charenzve harvested 350 bags of maize, 90 bags of cotton, 50 bags of sunflower and 20 bags of beans. The majority of this crop she sold to Zimbabwe's Grain Marketing Board.

Unequal distribution of land was a major factor behind the struggle for Independence. Before Independence the five per cent of the population who were white owned the better half of the land. The 95 per cent of the population who were black were left with the remaining poor half.

The agreement which gave Zimbabwe Independence prevented the new government from settling landless black farmers on the large white owned farms except when the white farmers were willing to sell their land. Not only land was needed, but equipment, training and credit to help the new settlers during the first difficult years. In fact only 36,000 families like Mrs Charenzve's were resettled in the first six years of Independence. An impressive figure, but barely scratching the surface of the problem when one million families like Joyce's need more or better land.

Despite this lack of new land, and some devastating years of drought, peasant farmers in Zimbabwe, like Mrs Charenzve, are now selling far more grain than before Independence. The government offered high prices, and set up convenient buying points, and the grain rolled in. It gave Zimbabwe two problems: in the long run, a tremendous strain on the land in the communal areas, calling for faster land reform, and in the short run – grain mountains.

At the beginning of 1987 Zimbabwe had two million tonnes of grain in store. This formed a useful strategic reserve –

recognised as the key to agricultural recovery in the poorer areas of the Third World. Food security there, in the view of European voluntary aid agencies, must take precedence over the freedom of industrial farmers in Australia and the USA to expand their Third World markets. When major producers call for an end to import barriers, they are in danger of neglecting food security needs and ignoring the 'special and differential treatment' for developing countries which is an established feature of GATT.

some was needed to feed people like Joyce who had a poor harvest. Meanwhile in neighbouring Mozambique farming has been disrupted by fighting, leading to widespread famine. Despite its hungry neighbour, Zimbabwe has found it difficult to sell its grain. Neither Joyce's family nor neighbouring Mozambique can afford to buy it. The price of maize on the world market has been lower than the price Zimbabwe paid its farmers, so to sell there would mean a loss the government could not afford.

The global economy is weighted against agriculturally productive African nations. The EC and the USA dispose of surplus grain on the world market at subsidised prices, undercutting countries like Zimbabwe. Export subsidies offered to their own traders by the EC and the USA damage Zimbabwe's efforts to give its farmers a fair deal. However, EC governments have paid for some of Zimbabwe's maize to go to Mozambique as triangular food aid.

Fair world trade is needed to enable the Zimbabwe Government to continue to buy the crops produced by people like Mrs Charenzve. Are we prepared for fair trade?

Buyers appointed by Zimbabwe's Grain Marketing Board purchased most of Mrs. Charenzve's crop.

The demand for freer markets in farm trade has been growing since the World Bank published a major report on agriculture in 1986. The Bank argued that both industrialised and developing countries would gain from the higher world prices which freer trade would bring, although farmers in the North and consumers in the South would lose out.

Not all economists share this view. Many have sat at different computers, making different assumptions, and have obtained different results about what would happen to developing countries if farm subsidies were abolished. Such studies have two major limitations. One is that the gains and losses they predict are all fairly small compared with the scale of debt, aid and other financial flows between the South and the North. The second is that they only show the effects on countries and not on rich and poor people within those countries. For example, encouraging Zimbabwe to 'gain' more from increasing its production and export of beef would mean encouraging the larger commercial farmers

Developing countries should keep their right to impose taxes on cheap food imports

more than the small-holders. The Bank's view that freer trade would raise world prices and reduce dumping has also been challenged. Many in the aid agencies fear that a freer world market would further concentrate cheap food production and marketing in the hands of the big farm corporations. They claim higher world prices could be achieved through 'managed supply systems', that is by limiting production and export opportunities for the richer farmers while maintaining the incomes of small family farmers.

If the EC is willing to help the Third World to gain something from current world trade negotiations, it should follow three main principles:

● The major food producers need to phase out export subsidies and reduce production of surplus commodities which depress world prices. Export prices should not be allowed to fall below the costs of production in the exporting countries. Minimum world reference prices should be established. The low-income food-importing countries should be compensated for higher prices.

● Every developing country should have the right to decide its own level of food self-sufficiency and security. Developing countries should keep their right to impose anti-dumping measures, including border controls and taxes on cheap food imports.

● The EC should improve access to its markets for developing countries, in particular reducing tariffs on processed foods and guaranteeing access to tropical products and foods like fruit and vegetables which compete with the CAP.

If these principles sound idealistic, there are signs that public opinion in the EC would support them. An EC survey in 1987 found that:

– 85 per cent of people interviewed in the 12 EC countries

World food prices are artificially low

favoured the EC's helping the Third World to develop its own food production rather than using it as a dumping ground for surpluses.

– 51 per cent were in favour of reducing EC production so that more foodstuffs could be bought from the Third World.

– Only 38 per cent supported export subsidies.

In April 1989 GATT member countries completed their mid-term review of the Uruguay Round with an interim deal on farm trade. They have imposed a freeze on current levels of support to farmers until the end of the Round in December 1990. They will use the time until then to negotiate 'substantial progressive reductions in agricultural support and protection' to follow during the 1990s. The hardest bargaining is still to come, but the US call for elimination of all subsidies, including export subsidies, seems to be dead.

Critics of subsidised farming and higher food prices cannot make comparisons with world food prices because these are artificially low, largely as a result of protectionist policies pursued by industrialised countries. A better guide is the average cost of production. This naturally varies from country to country, and from region to region, even valley to valley. Most farmers and most governments would agree that marginal, low-cost farming needs support. The problem, as the CAP has shown in Europe, is how to reach a consensus on the regions concerned and how to avoid a universal policy which helps the larger farmers. Similarly, member countries of GATT must decide how to cut over-production without removing the world's capacity to respond to emergency.

Who are the International Agencies?

As well as GATT, described in Chapter Five, and the World Food Programme, in Chapter Six, several other international agencies have an impact on the food prospects of the poor. EC member states have 25 per cent of the voting power in the World Bank, which provides loans for long-term development projects in Third World countries. Its policies are often tied to those of the International Monetary Fund (IMF), which offers short-term loans to governments with budget problems. The World Bank and IMF together often impose strict conditions like cutting state spending, boosting exports, devaluation and privatisation.

35 per cent of the debts of African, Caribbean and Pacific countries are owed to the IMF and the World Bank.

The International Fund for Agricultural Development (IFAD) also offers loans but on easy terms and specifically for small farmers' projects. The Food and Agriculture Organisation (FAO) is the main food policy arm of the United Nations and the World Food Council is a forum for the world's food ministers. The United Nations Conference on Trade and Development (UNCTAD) tries to assist the trade of Third World countries, in particular through schemes to stabilise their export earnings.

CHAPTER SIX

Food Aid

"Food aid, without assisting us to improve our production, is fertiliser for a rich crop called hunger. It is a contradiction in terms. Food donations are most welcome but, where they are not part and parcel of a programme to make the peasant farmer self-reliant in food production, they have been a handicap rather than a help."
(President Kaunda of Zambia, speaking at the World Food Conference 1988)

Food aid is the result of the surplus disposal policies of industrialised countries. In 1954 the USA passed its Public Law 480 setting up a food aid programme based on grants and credit. The original US motives were to encourage farm exports and to hold onto allies during the Cold War; part of the programme was renamed Food for Peace. The USA gradually encouraged other donor countries to share the costs and in the late 1960s the EC, whose Common Agricultural Policy was in its infancy, began its own food aid programme. More than three-quarters of food aid worldwide is now given free.

Agriculture ministries have always called the tune in food aid but over the years efforts have been made to meet criticisms by turning food aid into more of an instrument for development. At the end of 1986 management of the EC programme was switched from agriculture officials to aid officials, priority was given to the speed of emergency actions and the scope was increased for purchasing food aid in developing countries. But EC rules still demand that the majority of food aid 'should be mobilised on the Community market'.

"The objective of food self-sufficiency can only be achieved if food aid ultimately disappears."
(Final Recommendations of Sahel Cereals Conference, Cape Verde, 1986.)

Food aid from all donors cost nearly three billion dollars in 1987 and represented seven per cent of the cost of their aid programmes. For many years food aid has taken around 30 per cent of the European Commission's aid budget, reflecting its link with the CAP, but the proportion is lower in the aid budgets of the member states. Food aid is classed into three main types. Programme aid (54 per cent of total cereal aid in 1987-8) goes to governments, which either sell it on local markets or, in some countries, use it to pay civil servants. Project aid (27 per cent) goes to pay labourers on public works projects (food-for-work) or to nutrition schemes such as school feeding and mother and child health schemes. Only 19 per cent of food aid in 1987-8 fitted its television image and was delivered as emergency aid. But in sub-Saharan Africa the proportions were different: 41 per cent programme aid, 16 per cent project aid and 43 per cent emergency aid. The money raised from the sale of food aid has often been used to balance national budgets, but donors have favoured joint control of these funds to ensure that they are channelled into rural development.

13.2 million tonnes of cereal aid were shipped to developing countries in 1987-8, of which the EC supplied 19 per cent, making it the second largest donor after the USA (60 per cent). The total represented five per cent of developed countries' cereal stocks. 57 per cent of it went to Africa and the Middle East, 27 per cent to Asia and 16 per cent to Latin America and the Caribbean. In 1988 the EC supplied cereals to 53 countries, of which the top 10 were:

	Thousand tonnes
1. Bangladesh	302
2. Ethiopia	224
3. Egypt	160
4. Mozambique	148
5. Pakistan	63
6. Angola	45
7. Sri Lanka	40
Tunisia	40
9. Somalia	37
10. Madagascar	25

The other main type of food aid is dairy products (skimmed milk powder and butteroil). In 1981 the EC gave 68 per cent of all dairy aid, but in the mid-1980s the USA stepped up its shipments to account for 63 per cent by 1985 (EC 31½). EC

Food aid from the EC and the World Food Programme is delivered in Ethiopia.

Sebastiao Salgado/Magnum

Dairy aid accounts for nearly half the cost of EC food aid

dairy aid has been falling for some years now and the US interest in these products has slumped, too, following the rise in world milk prices. The bulk of the EC's dairy aid now goes to two large development schemes in India and China (see Box on Operation Flood). Dairy aid accounts for nearly half the cost of EC food aid.

Two international bodies are also active in food aid. The World Food Programme, founded in 1963, is the food aid agency of the United Nations. In the size of its resources, it is second only to the World Bank, showing the greater

Operation Flood

Most of the EC's dairy food aid has recently been used to help poorer countries develop their own dairy industries. The biggest and most controversial programme is Operation Flood in India. Between 1970 and 1985 the EC provided 366,000 tonnes of milk powder and 126,700 tonnes of butteroil to this programme, which is also backed by the World Bank. The aim was to increase the processing and delivery capacity of co-operatives of small rural producers in supplying India's major cities of Bombay, Calcutta, Delhi and Madras.

Milk powder and butteroil from the EC are reconstituted with local fresh milk and sold in the cities. Funds generated from the milk sales are invested in building large-scale dairy and cattle-feed plants and providing more milk tankers. Milk production has increased, though not dramatically, and through their co-operatives producers have gained a guaranteed market and a stable price. The European Commission sees Operation Flood as a successful

use of food aid as a tool for development.

But from the start Operation Flood had social as well as economic aims. It was intended to improve milk consumption among the rural poor and the incomes of small farmers and the landless. Its effects on the poor are less apparent. Increases in milk supply have gone mainly to richer city-dwellers who can afford it while women, who usually take care of the cattle, are rarely prominent in the co-operatives. Landless labourers, even if they own cattle, lack crop wastes to feed them and are unlikely to benefit without land reform. The richer producers have gained most. Funds from milk sales have gone mainly into modern dairy technology (another benefit for European suppliers) at the expense of local jobs, and not enough money has been ploughed into organising and training small milk producers.

When Operation Flood began, the recombined milk was cheaper than local fresh milk. This led to increased readiness of governments to provide food aid rather than money. It handles nearly one-quarter of the world's food aid, either from its own resources or as agent for donor governments. It specialises in development projects and emergency aid and is not involved in programme aid to governments. The Food Aid Convention, administered by the International Wheat Council, is a forum for pledging minimum quantities of cereal food aid. The EC, with a total pledge of 1,670,000 tonnes per year, the UK Government (whose share is 110,700 tonnes per year) and the Irish Government (whose share is 4,000 tonnes) are signatories to this Convention which guarantees an annual 7,517,000 tonnes from 11 donors.

Food aid, even when it is used for 'development' purposes, has come in for a number of criticisms:
● It can be a disincentive to local production, helping to

dependence on food aid and depressed the price for local producers, but pricing policy has now been put right. Dairy aid has also enabled local milk powder to be used for baby foods and luxury products, because food aid has made up the shortages. Another feature of Operation Flood is the cross-breeding of Indian cows with western animals to increase productivity. This is questionable because Indian cows and buffaloes are well-adapted to heat and humidity. Cross-bred cattle need better conditions and feed and are beyond the reach of the poorer farmers. Whilst EC dairy aid used to push milk prices down, the EC's use of animal feed exports from India increases feed prices for farmers there and competes for land with local food production for people and animals.

After much thought the EC decided in 1987 to go ahead with a new seven-year programme of 100,000 tonnes of dairy aid: a reduced rate of supply because India was already on the verge of self-sufficiency in milk. At the same

time the EC launched a similar scheme to supply China with 60,000 tonnes over five years to build up the dairy industry around 20 cities.

Yet critics continue to argue for an alternative dairy policy for India which is not based on the western model of processing and supply. It should instead improve traditional processing in the villages, to provide jobs and nutrition for the rural poor. The Indian buffalo may not have the highest yields, but it converts crop wastes and herbage most efficiently into milk and is a better source of draught-power. Cross-bred cattle often require green fodder and local cereals, and it is important that dairying should not make more demands on land needed for local food crops. Phasing out dairy aid and animal feed exports could improve the milk price to producers and lower their animal feed prices. According to researcher Shanti George, Indian dairying needs not so much a 'white revolution' as 'brown evolution'.

depress prices and discouraging policy changes needed to stimulate agriculture. The first part of this charge is not proven: studies of disincentives have been inconclusive. The second is more serious: food aid can add to the excuses which governments find to neglect their own food producers. Many governments have been slow in setting adequate farm prices. Others have failed to enforce necessary land reforms.

- It tends to create dependence on imports and on food not produced locally, such as wheat, or food which is difficult to market, such as milk.
- It does not always improve nutrition and in some forms can even be dangerous. If targeted at schools, food aid may not reach the very poorest, who do not attend school; there is also evidence that children who receive food aid in school are given less at home. The risks of incorrect use of milk powder (over-dilution, use of unsafe water) are well-known.
- Too little of it is reserved for emergencies. Until the African famine of 1984-5 less than 15 per cent of EC food aid went

---

Developing countries' total cereal imports in 1987-8 were 9 times greater than the cereals they received as food aid

---

to emergencies, and a special programme, the 'Dublin Plan' (named after the venue of the December 1984 European Summit), had to be created to respond to the African crisis.

- Its effectiveness can be eroded by long delivery times, deteriorating quality and other management problems. In 1986, donor promises exceeded by 208,000 tonnes the total needs of Sahelian countries: at the same time, following two good harvests, 200,000 tonnes of local surpluses remained unused. There is increasing use of 'multi-annual' food aid, with the risk that pledged food may arrive to compete with improved local harvests.
- It can be used as a political lever by donor and recipient governments, for example by the USA, in order to keep countries like Chile and Egypt in line with its own policies, or by Bangladesh to retain the loyalty of its public servants.
- It can displace more effective forms of aid in development budgets, such as cash for local farming.
- It is often given an inflated value. Food aid tends to be valued at what it costs in the protected markets of the

donor, which overstates its value at world market prices.

The EC has tried harder than the USA to respond to most of these criticisms and is now making efforts to integrate food aid into the development policies of the receiving countries.

But food aid is only the tip of the iceberg when it comes to food import dependence. Developing countries' total cereal imports in 1987-8 were nine times greater than the cereals they received as food aid. In sub-Saharan Africa cereal food aid was 40 per cent of total cereal imports in 1987-8. The extent of dependence by developing countries on imported grain is evidence of the success of the export promotion policies of major surplus producers. The USA in particular has used its food aid and concessional food sales to unlock markets.

The top 10 Third World wheat importers

	Million tonnes
1. China	17.0
2. Egypt	7.0
3. Algeria	3.3
South Korea	3.3
5. Iran	3.2
6. Iraq	2.8
7. Pakistan	2.5
8. India	2.1
9. Bangladesh	2.0
10. Indonesia	1.8

(Source: International Wheat Council forecast for 1988-9)

The EC has never had a programme of cheap food exports on the lines of the American PL 480 Scheme, but in 1988 the European Commission proposed one. The idea was to offer food on grant terms of about 40 per cent, leaving the developing countries to obtain loans on the money markets, guaranteed by the EC, for the remaining 60 per cent. The proposal was aimed at the middle-income countries of North Africa, rather than the poorest countries, and was designed to recover markets there from the Americans. The idea did not, however, go down well with EC member states. Increasing Third World debt to purchase food from Europe hardly fits the new approach of 'food aid for development'. If there is no alternative to sending food from the North, many would prefer the option of classical food aid.

Current FAO rules do not allow a poor country to ease its balance of payments by replacing its commercial imports with food aid; they only allow it to use food aid over and above normal imports and thus to become even more dependent on them once it has paid for its regular supplies. These rules were first evolved in the 1950s in the interests of richer exporting countries, and have been widely described as an anachronism, partly because no-one can estimate for certain what the 'normal' level of a country's imports would be without food aid. They should be replaced, perhaps by a new code of conduct on food aid, provided this is not used by donors to create loopholes for more surplus disposal.

There has been positive thinking in triangular operations and regional food security

There has been some positive thinking as well, in the growing priority given to triangular operations and regional food security. When a developing country runs out of food, some is often available in a neighbouring country. In a triangular operation a donor country pays for surplus food from one developing country to be delivered to another. These operations have the advantages of encouraging

---

Paying Peter to feed Paul

EC countries bought a total of 540,050 tonnes of cereal food aid in developing countries in 1987–8. Of this, the European Commission paid for 190,288 tonnes and the Netherlands 161,422 (UK 46,050).

The European Commission's 1988 food aid programme included triangular operations and local purchases in various products. Among the largest purchases were:

- 26,311 tonnes of white maize from Zambia to Malawi
- 12,160 tonnes of white maize from Kenya to Mozambique
- 34,360 tonnes of sorghum bought and delivered in Sudan
- 11,400 tonnes of rice from Thailand to Vietnam
- 6,540 tonnes of beans bought and delivered in Thailand
- 5,000 tonnes of beans from Argentina to Nicaragua.

Many refugees from fighting in Mozambique were among those receiving food aid in Malawi, and many Cambodian refugees in Thailand.

---

regional food trade, lessening transport delays and providing food more suited to local diets.

Triangular purchases are becoming more popular, though they are sometimes said to be more expensive or less readily available than developed country surpluses. In 1987-8, 8½ per cent of all cereal food aid consisted of triangular purchases or 'local' purchases (that is, a donor paying for

Chapati Parties get the Poor Back to Work

When floods struck Bangladesh in 1988, Norin Pandy and his family of five did not leave their house in the village of Harenahati. It was flooded for six weeks but they stayed on the roof. They have no land and, when the local rice crop was wiped out, they had to depend on the family's ration of 18 chapatis (pancakes) each day and some fishing: "If we didn't have chapatis, all the family would be dead, but after one month the land will be open again." Then Norin will be able to get work, earning 41 pence per day helping to restore the local crops of rice, jute and mustard.

The chapatis were the work of 150 volunteers in the village mobilised by Christian Aid's partner GK to maintain food supplies. In the darkness four big fires were blazing with chapatis frying on them and in the shadows dozens of people were mixing flour, kneading dough and rolling out chapatis. Between 4 pm and 11 pm on one day, the village produced 25,000 chapatis in this way. The flour is mainly government imported wheat flour, but Christian Aid's grant to GK helps pay for the organisation of many village groups, the cleaning of wells and ponds after the floods and seeds to help the farmers get back to work. The 'chapati parties' ensure that the wheat flour reaches the poor: uncooked wheat flour handed out after the disaster leads to selling and profiteering.

Flooding affects an estimated 550 million people in India and Bangladesh every year. Governments and international agencies meet to examine why Bangladesh is so prone to floods. Contractors wait for multi-million dollar schemes to be approved to divert or dredge rivers. Meanwhile, Christian Aid's partners are getting on with the job of helping village groups to survive the floods which have become a regular feature of their lives. GK is exploring canal-digging and small embankments. Another partner, Nijera Kori, is working to make 70,000 people more aware of their rights: for example, banks are legally obliged to give loans to people who can show a receipt for land bought under new land reform laws.

food bought and delivered within the same country). In 1987-8 the EC financed 49 per cent of all triangular and local purchases, Japan 20 per cent and the USA two per cent. A variation on this is the 'swap' arrangement by which a donor provides a country with food aid in wheat (which can be used for urban consumers) in return for its releasing local cereal stocks to needy groups. EC food aid managers now have the power to spend a small part of their budget on aid to local food production, once they know that regular food aid supplies will not be needed.

The Sahel countries of West Africa have been considering a regional scheme of 'food insurance' to replace traditional food aid. Donors would guarantee to supply food aid over a period of years, with deliveries adjusted each year to local harvests and conversion of food aid to financial aid when-ever the region could feed itself. A similar regional scheme has been thought up by the states in Southern Africa. Here the reserve would not be a physical food stock but a fund able to purchase up to 356,000 tonnes of grain, chiefly from surpluses in Zimbabwe and Malawi, in the case of a general food shortage in the region. The scheme would also promote grain trade within the region through training in market management and food security. Donors have so far been cautious, perhaps because the idea shifts decision-making powers even further from the food aid centres of the North.

Aid in dairy products should be considered quite separately from cereals. Dairy aid has gone up and down with

Dairy products are not essential

donor preferences and world prices. Both the EC and the USA are giving less than before and this trend is likely to continue as long as prices remain high. Dairy products are not essential. Many societies have alternative protein sources to milk – or use vegetable rather than animal oils – provided that adequate staple foods can supply a basis of protein energy. In a number of developing countries, milk products are undesirable imports owing to the risks of reconstituted milk powder, allergies to cow's milk and the danger that mothers will be persuaded to substitute baby milks for breast milk, despite the World Health Organisation's 1981 Code. Neither Ireland nor the UK supplies dairy food aid from its own budget. The virtual disappearance of the EC milk lake and butter mountain offers the EC an opportunity to bring dairy aid to an end.

Cereal food aid is another matter. The International Wheat Council forecasts that, even with increased production by small farmers, the position of developing countries in cereals is likely to worsen before it improves. Low-income developing countries meet one-fifth of their cereal import needs with food aid. The IWC estimates that, just to maintain that proportion up to the year 2000, they would have to increase their food aid two-fold. Between 1987 and 1989 world wheat prices nearly doubled, increasing the food import bill of many indebted countries.

One answer is to switch from imported wheat (eaten mainly in cities) to cereals which can be home-grown. In 1987 Nigeria, hitherto sub-Saharan Africa's biggest wheat importer, banned imports of wheat, rice, maize and barley. But there are bound to be shortfalls and some emergency needs while this kind of switch is being made. Food aid

Food aid budgets for cereals need to remain in existence as a safety net

budgets for cereals therefore need to remain in existence as a safety net, especially for chronic food importers like Egypt and Bangladesh which will need time to adjust to higher world prices.

Food aid donors should encourage the progressive reduction of food aid from the North, replacing it with triangular operations and aid to local food production. Cereal food aid should include a stated preference for local or regional supplies. This would stimulate production of staple foods in the Third World and promote regional food trade. An act of will is now required of the EC and the USA, as well as of some Third World governments who have come to depend on the balance of payments support and counterpart funds they receive from food aid. The objective must be to ensure that small farmers in developing countries are encouraged to move towards self-sufficiency in basic grains which will make food aid and grain imports less necessary.

CHAPTER SEVEN

The Use of the Land

"Now I know why I'm so bound up with my land. If someone takes a piece of my land, it's like tearing out a piece of my body. That's why the Bible says man was made of the clay of the earth. How can anyone live without land?"
(Brazilian peasant on hearing the Genesis story, quoted by Marcello de Barros Zouza)

At the height of the famine in 1984-5, British shoppers were shocked to see Ethiopian melons on their market stalls. A few months later a European meat marketing company carried out a careful survey to find out whether corned beef from Ethiopia would be accepted by British consumers. In the year ended September 1984, Ethiopia exported over £1½ million of linseed cake, cottonseed cake and rapeseed meal for livestock in the European Community.

These products would not have replaced the grain that Ethiopia needed, but the question remained. Should countries which have large numbers of hungry people use prime land to grow export crops? The thought is an uncomfortable one, but economists tell us that the poorest countries need foreign exchange earnings and that, if their land is suited to growing products attractive to richer countries, they may do better to export and use the earnings to import more food for their people.

"We've always been ordinary farmers. I'm the son of a farmer. But with the arrival of colonisation, we started to specialise. From then on, my father planted coffee and cocoa only. In the end we even had to buy our bananas elsewhere."
(Mgr Bernard Agre, Bishop of Man, Ivory Coast, 1989)

The criticism of export crops is shared by many peasant groups in the Third World who question why their countries need to export to the extent they do. Isn't this policy forced on them by the International Monetary Fund and the World Bank, who want to see them pay off their external debt? "Increasing exports to escape from economic crisis is not in the interest of small farmers and the poor, who should develop internal markets for food," peasant groups say. "Liberalisation of markets is only of interest to the multinationals." Lloyd Timberlake sums up the pressure to export and the resulting debt trap in a gruesome analogy: "If children are dying, more – not less – children are needed. And, if crop prices are falling, more – not less – cash crops are needed."

How has it come about that people in poor countries use so much of their land to produce food for other people to eat? Colonial history gives us the first clue. Up to colonial times semi-arid areas of Africa had a mix of food crops, trees and livestock, with intercropping and crop rotation. Then specialisation was introduced by the colonial powers and quickly adopted by farmers tempted by the attractive prices offered for export crops.

Since the 1960s multinational companies and local landowners have taken over where the colonial powers left off. Many cash crops, such as new varieties of palm oil and 'dollar bananas' (see Box, page 69), are grown on plantations controlled by multinationals. Most international farm trade is

Landowners have found it more profitable to produce for export

in the hands of a small number of companies: three banana companies control 80 per cent of world trade, three cocoa companies control 83 per cent and three tea companies have 85 per cent of their respective markets. Of the top 100 agro-industrial companies, 25 are British. Consumers in industrialised countries spend over 200 billion dollars per year on Third World farm products but traders, processors and marketers get most of the benefit. Of the 10 pence we pay for a banana in the shops, only one penny is returned to the grower.

Even where multinational interests are not involved, landowners have found it more profitable to produce for export. Central American beef exports in the 1970s rose 448 per cent, while beef consumption per person in the region declined by 14 per cent. Mexican farmers can make 20 times more growing tomatoes for export than producing food for Mexicans. At the time of famine in Sudan in 1985, sorghum producers continued to export their crop as fodder for animals in Saudi Arabia. It is when the poor and hungry cannot afford to buy food that richer producers in developing countries switch to more lucrative markets abroad.

Christian Aid/Stuart Franklin

Workers picking pineapples at a large Del Monte plantation in

Mindanao, the Philippines. Who benefits?

Brazil, by far the biggest Third World exporter of farm products to the EC, was in 1985-6 the world's leading exporter of soya cake and oil, coffee and orange juice. If more of their own people could afford to buy food, countries like Brazil might not have such large surpluses to export.

Yet, if the fundamental need is to increase rural purchasing power, how are farmers to live except by selling their

'Is there the right balance between cash crops and food crops?'

produce? The argument against cash crops comes full circle if the rural poor have no other way of raising their incomes. Two important questions are 'Who benefits?' and 'Is there the right balance between cash crops and food crops?' There are no simple answers to these questions. An interesting example is the Philippines. Palm oil (like sugar) in the Philippines is a plantation crop, but coconut oil is not. 700,000 small farmers in the Philippines grow coconut oil and as much as 25 per cent of the people depend on it in some way (growing, processing, transporting, marketing). Yet coconut oil export earnings have already fallen and the real palm oil boom (from high-yielding palms developed in Unilever's laboratories) is still to come. Peasant export production is often a high-risk option because of the research power of multinationals which tends to work against the interests of small uncontrolled producers.

The greater the success of peasant exports, the more vulnerable they become to disruption or even retaliation in international trade. Cassava (also known as tapioca or manioc), grown in Thailand's dry and poor north-east by over two million peasant families and now largely exported for European livestock, is an example of a small-holder cash crop which has not displaced the main food crop, rice, because cassava is grown on higher ground. The crop was so successful that the EC imposed a 'voluntary' quota on Thailand of 5.5 million tonnes per year and asked the country to find some alternative crops.

On the other hand, in Brazil, soya and coffee grown for export have taken land from the beans and maize grown to feed the people. The table overleaf gives a few examples to show that export crops can benefit the poor, but it depends on who grows them and what effect they have on food production.

Noi Petsri is a 55-year-old farmer in Sanarm Chaikhet, 100 miles from Bangkok, Thailand. "We were very poor 20 years ago. Then tapioca brought good years. For the first time there was money for food and a little more. We made our houses stronger. Clothes from the village for my children. All seven could go to school. Books. Two bicycles to take them. We don't have TV, but we have radio, and it was the radio which told us tapioca had become a bad crop. Now we are getting only 0.9 baht (2.4p) per kilo; once it was 4.5 baht. I don't know where Brussels is exactly. I don't understand why they tell me to grow mango or eucalyptus. Such things take years to give a good crop. Meanwhile how do we eat?"

Photo by permission of the British Library

There is one further pitfall in the snakes-and-ladders game which Third World farmers are forced to play. Having made so many Third World economies dependent on their export crops, the richer countries are now finding substitutes, using the latest biotechnology to find alternatives to tropical products. The best-known example is sugar. Cheap maize surpluses in the USA led to the development of High Fructose Corn Syrup as an artificial sweetener. The USA has cut its

The richer countries are now finding substitutes

sugar import quotas from three million tonnes to around one million today. This decision is directly linked to the 66 per cent malnutrition found recently among children on the Philippine sugar-producing island of Negros. EC quotas restricting the use of artificial sweeteners have prevented them from taking too much of the market away from sugar, but these measures are aimed mainly at protecting the European sugar beet industry, which has itself dumped large surpluses on the markets for Third World sugar cane.

Some EC countries now permit the manufacture of chocolate in which vegetable fats partly replace cocoa butter, a major source of income for one in four people in Ghana, with the prospect that 1992 will bring commercial pressures on

65

the remaining cocoa importers to fall into line. Real vanilla can now be produced by bacteria in laboratories, without a plant and without a farmer: bad news for 70,000 farmers in four island countries like Madagascar who depend on the vanilla crop. Substitution of Third World products in the biotech laboratories of the North makes reliance on export crops extremely hazardous, even in cases where the benefits do currently go to small farmers.

Cash crops: Who benefits?

CROP	PRODUCER COUNTRY	WHO GROWS IT?	WHO MARKETS IT?	WHO PROCESSES IT?
SOYA	BRAZIL	Big Farmers and Family Farmers	Grain Companies and Co-ops	Multinationals, Private Companies and Co-ops
SUGAR	BRAZIL	Plantation Owners	State and Private Companies	Private Companies
SUGAR	PHILIPPINES	Plantation Owners	Private Companies	Private Companies
COCONUTS	PHILIPPINES	Small Farmers	Private Companies	Private Companies
PALM OIL	MALAYSIA	State and Private Plantations	Private Companies	Private Companies
PEANUTS	SENEGAL	Big and Small Farmers	State Monopoly until 1988; now Private	Private Companies
CASSAVA	THAILAND	Small Farmers	One Main Company	Private Companies
COFFEE	BRAZIL	Plantation Owners and Family Farmers	State and Private Companies	Multinationals and Private Companies
COCOA	GHANA	95% Small Farmers	State Marketing Agency	Multinationals and State Marketing Agency
TEA	SRI LANKA	54% State Plantations; rest Private	Mainly Privately Auctioned	State and Private Companies
ORANGES	BRAZIL	Big Farmers	Two Main Companies	Two Main Companies
BANANAS	WINDWARD ISLANDS	Small Farmers	Multinationals	—

If the poor are to benefit, Third World countries must therefore give more priority to domestic food crops, not export-led agriculture, however much pressure the IMF tries to put on them.

Even export cropping by small-holders may turn out to be like cheap food imports – a short-term fix with no future. But farmers do not need to have their crop exported in order to get a cash income from it. In many countries it would be

MONOCROPPED, ROTATED OR INTERCROPPED?	EFFECT ON FOOD PRODUCTION	MAIN EXPORT DESTINATION	WORLD MARKET PROSPECTS
Monocropped, some rotated with Wheat	Takes Productive Land, Government Loans & Advanced Technology	EC	Over-supply
Monocropped	Uses most Productive Land in Central Brazil and North-East	Motor Fuel and Home Consumption	Over-supply and Substitution
Monocropped	Uses Productive Land	USA	Over-supply and Substitution
Intercropped	Does not compete with Food Crops	USA	General over-supply of Oil Crops
Monocropped	Uses Peat Soils, not most Productive Land	India, China, Pakistan	General over-supply of Oil Crops
Intercropped, Rotated and Monocropped	Productive Land shared with Basic Food Crops	France	General over-supply of Oil Crops
Intercropped with Sugar	Does not compete with Rice	EC	Over-supply; EC quota
Monocropped	Takes Productive Land	USA	Over-supply
Intercropped and Monocropped	Productive Land shared with Basic Food Crops	UK	Over-supply
Monocropped	Tea has impoverished the Land	Egypt, Iraq, UK	Moderate over-supply
Monocropped	Takes Productive Land	USA	Demand still rising
Intercropped	Productive Land shared with Basic Food Crops	UK	Competition from Lower-cost Plantation Bananas

Washing bananas on the island of Dominica. What future for Caribbean banana growers when markets are opened up after 1992?

Philip Wolmuth

sufficient for them to recover markets in their towns and cities which are still being weaned onto food imports. Delegates to the Sahel Cereals Conference in 1986 hit the right note when they resolved that 'Food crops should become cash crops'. Farming communities need to be

---

One billion people in rural areas have no land, or almost no land, of their own

---

encouraged by the right prices to produce more than they consume – of the foods eaten locally.

Farmers can only do this if they have enough land. Export crops have been one major, though by no means the only, reason for unfair land distribution in much of the Third World. One billion people living in rural areas of the Third World have no land, or almost no land, of their own. Women, who do the majority of farm work, own only a tiny fraction of the land in their own right. Over half of the landless are in India and Bangladesh: 10 per cent of

A Box of Bananas

A tussle is looming as 1992 approaches between 'dollar bananas' from plantations in Central America and higher-cost bananas from the UK's traditional source of supply, the Windward Islands. Under present trade rules agreed with the group of African, Caribbean and Pacific (ACP) countries, the UK and five other EC countries limit the import of cheaper dollar bananas in order to guarantee duty-free markets for their traditional suppliers. Belize, Surinam and the English-speaking Caribbean islands provide seven out of ten bananas eaten in the UK; Cameroun, Ivory Coast and the French Caribbean islands supply France; and Somalia supplies Italy. 1992, the year of the Single Internal Market, will outlaw national quotas in the EC.

Central American states have advantages in land and climate for low-cost production over Caribbean islands, but their bananas are also grown on plantations, some of them controlled by American multinationals. Caribbean bananas are grown mainly by small family farmers. Dollar bananas are sold to Germany duty-free for two-thirds of the price at which Caribbean bananas enter the UK, and plantation managers in Central America are already talking of widening this price gap and squeezing out the 'inefficient' producers.

Even the 20 per cent duty which most EC countries charge on dollar bananas will not be enough to cancel out their cost advantage. If Caribbean bananas had to compete on equal terms with dollar fruit after 1992, the main source of jobs and income in St Lucia, Dominica, St Vincent and much of Grenada would disappear, causing economic and social disaster. No other crop has yet been found which could give these islands the same level of employment and earnings.

A solution has to be found which honours the EC's treaty promises to its traditional suppliers. A quota, as well as the 20 per cent duty, could be placed on dollar bananas entering the whole EC market, or a minimum import price could be fixed at a level which cancels out the price difference. Completely free trade would wipe out the jobs of small family farmers in regions where Europe has historical and legal obligations.

Where Bananas in the EC come from

| Grown in the EC and its Territories | Africa, Caribbean & Pacific | Dollar bananas (Central and South America) |

Bangladeshi landowners control 50 per cent of the land and 50 per cent of the cattle, while nearly 50 per cent of the population are landless. The food-producing resources of Bangladesh could be better developed if farmers had more access to them. Too many of them are farmworkers or tenants who have little or no incentive to invest in their land. In India one per cent of landowners control 20 per cent of the land and nearly half the population suffer from malnutrition. The proportion of malnourished in China, on the other hand, is around three per cent, but in China land cannot be bought or sold; most rural Chinese have access to food-producing resources.

In the African drylands over-cultivation, rather than land shortage, has been the major problem of land use; peasants have a traditional right of use rather than legal possession. But

Feeding the Animals

Farm animals, like humans, have their fast food. Although 58 per cent of animal feed in the EC comes from grass and 23 per cent from raw cereals, the rest consists of compound feeds. The EC is the world's largest buyer of animal feeds, importing 40 million tonnes in 1985. 60 per cent of cereals and other feedstuffs for animals come from developing countries. This is because they are cheaper than home-produced grain or oilseeds. In the 1960s the EC and other trading nations agreed not to tax the import of 'cereal substitutes'. This has been a benefit to some Third World farmers and traders, and to European farmers who get cheap feed, but a problem for the European Commission which is left with more surpluses of home-grown cereals.

Half the feed imports consist of soya and cassava. Next in order of importance are maize gluten (mainly from the USA), molasses, citrus and beet pulp, bran, sunflower and fishmeal. The EC's reliance on soya began with US aid to increase European meat production in the 1950s and 1960s: showing how easy it is for countries to slide into dependence on imported inputs for their food production.

Of the EC's imports of feedstuffs from the Third World, Brazil supplies 33 per cent. Brazil, the USA and Argentina provided most of the 13 million tonnes of soya imports in 1985. From the 1960s Brazilian farmers were encouraged by their government and by multinationals to plant soya, which for many became their only crop and exhausted the soil as both the nation and its farmers struggled to cope with growing debts.

90 per cent of the EC's cassava imports in 1985 came from Thailand, where three million people, farmers and processors, depend on the crop. Although it can place only a minimal import tax on cassava, the 'voluntary' quota which the EC imposed on Thailand in 1982 is estimated to have cost the country £100 million per year in lost exports. Yet the aid package offered by the EC as compensation amounted to £32 million over five years. Like soya, cassava can wear out the soil if it is overfarmed.

Several animal feed imports (soya, sunflower and palm kernel cake) are jointly produced with vegetable oils, in which tropical producers face great competition on the world market. West African palm oil exports are in decline but plantations in the Far East, especially in Malaysia, are approaching a boom. At the same time the EC has been trying to

in Brazil two per cent of the landowners have 60 per cent of the arable land, at least half of which lies idle. Yet 12 million rural day workers in Brazil remain landless. Many Brazilian farmers have been dispossessed to make way for coffee, tobacco or ranching. The problem of inequity in land ownership is not confined to the Third World: the Brazilian pattern (two per cent owning 60 per cent of the land) is also true of Andalusia in Southern Spain, where 400,000 farm workers are unemployed for much of the year. The apartheid system in South Africa keeps 85 per cent of the population on the

EC Imports of Animal Feeds 1985

reach self-sufficiency in oilseeds, by means of production aids to rapeseed, sunflower and soya, at much greater cost than if it simply imported tropical oils. A 1987 proposal for a tax on oils and fats to help pay these support costs would have favoured domestic oilseeds and butter, but it was rejected by EC Ministers.

Changes in the animal feed and vegetable oil markets are closely related. There is already pressure from European farmers and the European Commission for GATT to allow taxes on imported cereal substitutes. This would make home-grown cereals more competitive with imported feeds. Demand for animal feeds may fall as livestock numbers decrease with milk quotas. The EC's aim of self-sufficiency in oilseeds is both costly and harmful to Third World oil producers. But its readiness to import cheap animal feeds has encouraged some Third World farmers to rely on a single export crop and exhaust their soils. The answer is not new restrictions but a new priority in the Third World for food production and local animal feed industries.

worst 14 per cent of the land and has forcibly removed an estimated 3.5 million people from their homes.

Landlessness has been caused by feudal land tenure systems, scarcity of land in densely populated areas and

Movement to marginal land has often damaged the environment

relegation of the poor to marginal lands when colonial governments and multinationals moved in. Movement to marginal land has often damaged the environment. In the Andes, Indian peasants driven out of valleys by colonists have cultivated mountain slopes liable to erosion. In Ethiopia, the Awash River basin has been exploited by foreign companies cultivating cotton and sugar cane. Forced back onto less fertile lands, the herds of the Afar pastoralists have seriously overgrazed them.

Small farmers can make better use of their land than big landowners. A study in 1979 concluded that in North-East Brazil redistribution of land into small-holdings could raise output by 80 per cent. In countries like Japan, China, Nicaragua and Zimbabwe, where land reform has been carried out, food production and yields have risen. In Zimbabwe's case the increase in peasant production has also been due to incentives given to small-holders. Elsewhere land reform has often been introduced but with little effect. Governments have wilted under pressure from landlords and reforms have been incomplete.

Landowners have been among the best organised and most ruthless elements in Third World societies. Every other day since 1984, Brazilian landowners have murdered on average one person working for land reform (peasants, lawyers, priests). Three days before Christmas 1988, Chico Mendes, president of the Xapuri rural workers' union in Brazil, and a Christian Aid partner, was brutally shot. Chico had led groups of rubber-tappers, agricultural workers whose live-lihoods preserved rather than destroyed the Amazon rainforest, through non-violent confrontations with ranchers at sites in the forest which they wanted to clear for pasture. His 'crime' was to defend rural workers and the forest environment against the plundering and destructive landowning class, in a country where export farming has been given priority over food production through fair shares of land.

With other leaders and in other countries besides Brazil,

Chico's struggle will go on. In the words of a Christian gathering in Brazil in 1986: "The struggle for land isn't just a question of economics. It's a struggle for the dignity of people, who demand to be recognised as daughters and sons of God. So the land is more than a piece of ground. It is the gift of God, the place of work and of life." If we had the option of offering a hungry family a sack of grain, a packet of seeds or a plot of land, we would have to begin with the land. For many people secure land tenure is the most fundamental asset required to bring about an end to hunger.

CHAPTER EIGHT

Food Production and Rural Incomes

"Third World consumers can buy food, however cheap, only if they have incomes, and for the great majority of them the only source of income is farming."
(Tony Hill, Catholic Institute for International Relations, 1986)

After the Second World War the USA launched its Marshall Plan of economic aid to Europe, also known as the European Recovery Programme. This aid was an essential and much appreciated boost to countries ravaged by war. But if the USA had gone further and had guaranteed indefinite supplies of cheap food, the effect on farmers in Europe would have been disastrous. Many more would have lost their livelihoods, rural areas would have been depopulated faster and Western Europe would soon have become dependent on food imports.

If food production in the Third World were to suffer in this way the effect would be even more devastating, because in

---

Farmers' incomes need to be raised by restoring the supply of food from rural areas to the towns

---

low-income countries farmers make up 70-80 per cent of the workforce, earning income not just from farming but from a range of related activities. It is their incomes and their jobs that would be lost – and their hunger which would follow. The reason for helping the Third World's small farmers is not simply to help them grow more food but to increase the incomes of the majority of the population.

Above all, farmers' incomes need to be raised by restoring the supply of food from rural areas to the towns. The fact that European food aid is sent to 67 countries does not mean that as many as 67 countries are unable to feed themselves. It is more likely to mean that city-dwellers in those countries have become dependent on imported wheat. An EC report sums it up: "The rural world is self-sufficient but is not generating the necessary surplus to feed the towns, which are being increasingly supplied from the international market."

Why has aid to Third World farming failed to increase rural incomes and left so many people hungry in the rural areas? Why is there a drift of people to the towns? At least three types of farming have been tried in the Third World: Green Revolution, collectivised and peasant farming.

High yielding wheat seed ready for planting in Maharashtra State, India. But can the poorest families afford either the seeds or the crop?

75

In the 1960s and 1970s the Green Revolution in some Asian countries dramatically increased yields from improved seeds, especially in fertile regions such as the Indian Punjab. But the seeds were wheat and rice, and poor farmers who grew maize, sorghum, millet or beans did not benefit. Nor did

The Green Revolution widened the gap between rich and poor

most of those with little land. The Green Revolution depended on expensive irrigation as well as on fertilisers and pesticides appropriate to the new seeds. The hybrid seeds supplied were of a type that farmers have to buy from the suppliers every year, abandoning the age-old practice of using seeds saved from the last harvest. Although yields increased, so did farm costs. It was the bigger and better-off farmers who benefited most from the Green Revolution – as did the multinationals and developed countries which had produced the new packages of inputs. In India and the Philippines the increased production replaced food imports, but left most of the poor with no more food to eat. The Green Revolution further concentrated land ownership and widened the gap between rich and poor. As a technical solution, it left the problem of equity unsolved.

Collectivised farming has not solved either the food production or the hunger problem, but it has taken a large share of government investment. FAO reported in 1982 that only eight per cent of Ethiopia's agriculture budget went to small farmers: the rest went to state farms. State farms in Mozambique have in some years taken over 90 per cent of the agriculture budget as well as much of the peasants' land, although since 1984 there has been a shift towards 'family' farms. China and Vietnam have also re-introduced a measure of family farming after earlier experience with collective farms.

There have also been attempts in Africa to set up large-scale peasant farming projects but hunger has persisted on Sudan's huge Gezira cotton scheme and on Kenya's Mwea rice scheme because the workers have low incomes and cannot grow all the food crops they need. Investing all resources in a single crop has been one of the great mistakes of aid projects and Green Revolution farming: it flies in the face of traditional agriculture which is based on mixed farming and intercropping.

More success has been seen where aid has been given

directly to peasant farming. Credit, inputs, favourable prices and minor land reforms after independence in Zimbabwe enabled peasants' maize deliveries to rise from four per cent of the total national output in 1979-80 to a remarkable 55 per cent of the total in 1986. Yet despite this success, it is the richer peasant farmers who have benefited most. Only 15 per cent of peasants in communal areas – the richer ones who can be relied upon to repay – receive credit, and only 10 per cent farm the best land which provides the bulk of the maize.

If these approaches have often failed to make an impact on hunger, what new thinking is needed? The focus of support should be on increasing the incomes of small farmers in the

---

The focus of support should be on increasing the incomes of small farmers in low-resource areas

---

low-resource areas, so that their incomes can rise simultaneously with food production. The type of farming matters: it is sometimes called agro-ecology, and it has the following features.

- It is based on the traditional techniques of mixed farming (crops and animals), crop rotations and intercropping. This interdependence reduces the risk of harvest failure. The people of Haiti, who lost all their pigs to swine fever in 1983, have pleaded for the return of their traditional 'Creole pigs', a hardy breed which survived on crop wastes, rather than the sophisticated breeds offered by the USA which require imported animal feeds, buildings and more veterinary care, most of them beyond the purse of the Haitian peasant.

- It relies on traditional staple foods, especially drought-resistant grains (sorghum and millet more than maize, rice or wheat). The problem for African farmers in supplying their towns is shown by the difference in diet between a peasant in Senegal, who eats on average 158 kg of local millet and 19 kg of rice per year, and a citizen of the capital, Dakar, who consumes 77 kg of imported rice, 33 kg of imported wheat and just 10 kg of millet. Root crops like cassava and legumes like peas and beans have been neglected as a source of nutrition.

- It is usually rainfed farming, which comprises 80 per cent of the world's cultivated land, but has received less attention than irrigation. In the world's dryland areas, irrigation, if it is to benefit the poor, is usually more successful in village-level market gardening than in grandiose dam projects which transform whole farming systems.

- It is more organic, relying on natural inputs more than imported chemicals and equipment. Organic farming has a potential for growth without creating more debt.
- It applies science to improve rather than displace traditional farming, starting from the systems that farmers know and seeing how science can help realise their potential. This potential for growth is greater than for industrial or Green Revolution farming.

Types of Agriculture: Current Production and Sustainable Potential for Production

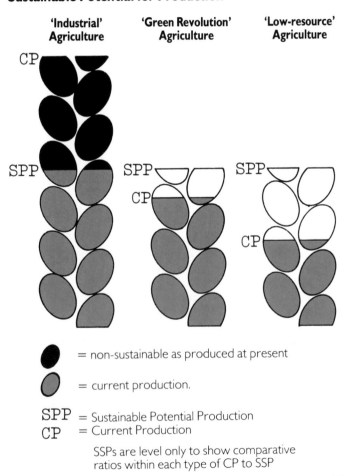

| 'Industrial' Agriculture | 'Green Revolution' Agriculture | 'Low-resource' Agriculture |

● = non-sustainable as produced at present

◐ = current production.

SPP = Sustainable Potential Production
CP = Current Production

SSPs are level only to show comparative ratios within each type of CP to SSP

Features of Sustainable Agriculture in the Tropics

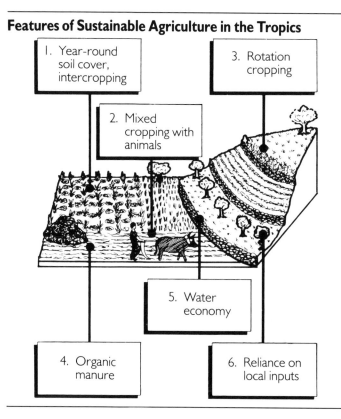

1. Year-round soil cover, intercropping

2. Mixed cropping with animals

3. Rotation cropping

4. Organic manure

5. Water economy

6. Reliance on local inputs

- It is sustainable. It protects the soil, and safeguards the resources of the land for future generations.
- It is the type of farming most often carried out by women, especially in Africa. A UN survey in 1985 suggested that small-holdings were essentially a women's farming system. On the other hand, only $3\frac{1}{2}$ per cent of Africa's agricultural extension workers, who carry out village level training, are female. Women also receive less technical advice and credit than men.
- It is often unpopular with those who exercise power. There is an array of forces pulling in the opposite direction, including urban populations (wanting cheap or imported food), multinationals (who want the best land) and sometimes agriculture officials out of touch with the small farmer.

Small-holder farming, or 'low-resource farming' by small farmers, can only develop if it has the right incentives, from both public and private sectors. There must first be a conscious decision by governments to divert funds from

Jenny Matthews

Pick of the crop: a Guatemalan widow digging in order to plant banana trees. Small-holder farming is often women's work.

export crops and big farming schemes towards small-holder farming and local staple crops.

Then research and planning need to be undertaken by consulting the farmers themselves. "Nyerere is right," said a Tanzanian extension worker in 1977. "So-called leaders do entirely too much *talking* to the peasants. No one ever wants to *listen* to them." There has been too little research into techniques for small-holders and into their own food crops. Training and credit need to be made much more widely available, not only for richer farmers and not only for men. Seeds, tools, fertilisers and pesticides should where possible be produced locally, to reduce dependence on imports, and may need to be subsidised or given on credit.

Much of this swims against the tide of advice from donors like the IMF and the World Bank, whose policies often require budget cuts, the withdrawal of subsidies and the transfer of farm services to the private sector. While many state agencies have been inefficient and would gain from competition, the total withdrawal of the state from Third World farming would be a disaster consigning the world's poorest people to the mercy of the market – or a vacuum if the private sector failed to fill the gap.

The state and the private sector have complementary roles in supporting small-holder farming. The role of the state should be to do what the market will not do. To encourage producers, it should establish floor and ceiling prices so that farmers do not have to cope with wild fluctuations of market prices. There are recent signs from countries like Ghana and Nigeria that higher producer prices are starting to revive small-holder farming. Stable prices also discourage black market and over-the-border trading which is seldom in the interest of the poorest consumers. Private markets move food away from areas of shortage if there is no purchasing power there. Public agencies must therefore retain a role in seeing

Clive Robinson

More village grain stores like this one in Zimbabwe will be needed if Africa is to reduce its crop losses after harvest.

81

Frits N Eisenloeffel

*Farmers who still have a pair of oxen for ploughing after the drought in Eritr
the revival of farming.*

have become the exception. Seeds, tools and oxen are indispensable for

that food reaches marginal areas and vulnerable groups.

The state also needs to improve the marketing of local food products in the towns, by upgrading transport and through job creation to restore purchasing power and strengthen the town/country trade link. Town dwellers need income to buy local farmers' produce, and farmers need consumer goods in the rural areas on which they can spend their money. In

More encouragement is needed for small-scale processing of traditional cereals

language familiar to EC policy-makers, the poorest countries need a more dynamic internal market.

More encouragement is needed for small-scale processing of traditional cereals. Millet dehuskers, for example, or new types of wheatless bread, by promoting local cereal consumption, can help developing countries meet more of their own food needs and reduce both poverty and hunger. Food fairs, like a recent one in Nicaragua's capital, Managua, at which 100 varieties of local beans were displayed, can do the same. In some African countries post-harvest losses of crops through poor storage and handling account for anything up to 25 per cent. Improvements need to be made in local storage capacity, at producer and trader level, for example in the encouragement of village cereal banks. Above village level storage capacities need to be developed, both physically in warehouses and financially by creating funds for food purchases. This would generally enable the state to avoid expensive centralised storage while remaining responsible for strategic reserves and purchases. A return to storage at producer level would be another return to traditional wisdom.

All these incentives can be provided by developing country governments and aid donors. For both, a change in priorities is involved. But, like a delicate plant, small-holder farming needs something more: a measure of protection from the excesses of agricultural trade. It can rarely grow unless the competition from cheap food imports is contained. Here the European Community faces both ways. In Niger the government provides protection for rice producers through an import tax and compulsory take-up of local production by the importing traders. There, and in Cameroun and Mali, the EC has helped the government establish systems of protection for rice-growers. On the other hand, the dumping of subsidised EC beef exports in Togo, in competition with live

Financial Times

Frying cassava flour in Nigeria: improved processing of traditional staple foods helps countries to be more self-sufficient.

cattle imports from neighbouring Sahelian countries, has prompted even the World Bank to recommend the Government of Togo to introduce an import tax to keep out cheap EC beef.

The Sahelian states' cereals conference in 1986 called for a protected regional market in West Africa which would discourage imports of rice and wheat and favour traditional cereals. Nigeria's ban on imports of wheat, rice, maize and

85

barley has, according to the *Financial Times*, "forced a return to traditional local staples such as yam, cassava, millet and sorghum, all of which have consequently seen a rise in producer prices. The ban has also increased domestic grain production and the entry of breweries, milling companies and food processors into the agricultural sector." The drift of large numbers of rural Nigerians to the cities has begun to slow down.

Policies of this kind, to protect Third World agriculture, lead to just the type of controls which the USA and Australia would ultimately like to abolish, to give export opportunities to their own low-cost farmers. In Europe these policies sometimes lead people to say that the principles and mechanisms of the CAP should be exported to developing countries. "Don't just scrap the CAP, export it too," said a *Guardian* leader in October 1985. Unfortunately, the *Guardian* missed its own point when it called for lower prices in the industrialised countries "at the expense only of the loss of some uneconomic farms" (for farms, read farmers). The main lesson of the CAP, that production levels can be raised even in marginal areas if government policies encourage producers through pricing, marketing and infra-

Any copying of the CAP in the Third World must ensure that benefits reach the poorest

structure, can be applied to the Third World's millions of neglected peasant farmers.

As always, there is a balance to be struck. Any copying of the CAP in the Third World must ensure that benefits reach the poorest and do not make the rich richer. "Policies intended to guarantee high prices to producers and stable prices for consumers may provide increased income to traders and large producers but not reach the majority of small producers and consumers." That could have been a comment on the CAP in Europe. It is, in fact, a recent verdict by the Open University on the Bangladesh grain market.

Even if they provide all these incentives, economists and governments will not achieve the revival of small-holder farming unless they take full account of the human element. Agricultural development means first and foremost the development of people in farming. The starting-point needs to be the wisdom and motivation of small farming communities themselves. That means consulting them properly

Agricultural development means first and foremost the development of people in farming

and working to promote and strengthen farmers' organisations, especially of women. Scattered Third World farmers are often weak in organisation, compared with their Northern counterparts and with city dwellers. Stronger farmers' organisations can give their members a voice; they are also an excellent vehicle for agricultural training. In the poorest and most remote communities, voluntary agencies and social action groups can reinforce farmers' organisations and provide a valuable channel for ideas as well as resources.

CHAPTER NINE

At the Grassroots

"The majority of the world's people have scarcely enough to keep them alive. They have little or no say in what happens to them. Unlike the strong they cannot protect or further their own interests. We cannot be content to alleviate their suffering. It must be brought to an end."
(Christian Aid's Statement of Commitment *To Strengthen the Poor,* July 1987)

Many of the projects in Africa, Asia and Latin America which Christian Aid helps to support aim to strengthen grassroots groups to increase food production and rural incomes. This chapter describes some of them. It is this type of group which Christian Aid has in mind when its Statement of Commitment goes on:

"We must act strategically to strengthen the arm of the poor until they can stand up to those who so often act against them, and have the power to determine their own development under God.
"If they are well nourished and in good health, they are stronger.
If they have land and can grow their own food, they are stronger.
If they can earn a living and have a measure of financial independence, they are stronger.
If they are self-reliant and self-sufficient, they are stronger.
If they are knowledgeable about the causes of their poverty, they are stronger.
If they are protected by just laws, they are stronger.
If they are organised to co-operate and act together, they are stronger.

"We cannot decide for the poor what it would mean to them to grow and develop as the sons and daughters of God. We must help to establish the pre-conditions

which allow them to determine their own development."

We in the North, for example, cannot 'decide' questions of land reform or farm pricing for peoples in the South, but we can support grassroots organisations which represent the interests of the poor in those policies. And we can monitor whether our own governments are pursuing policies which create the 'pre-conditions' for self-development.

"This strategy for justice is not ours. We must pursue it in partnership with the poor and all who stand by them."

By this, Christian Aid's Statement means that the priorities for action overseas must be decided by the organisations of the poor. Ecclesiastes reminded us (9.16): "No-one thinks of a poor man as wise or pays any attention to what he says." This we must try to reverse. Christian Aid does not run its own projects overseas. It works with partners, either local communities or the organisations which represent them, including church bodies and Christian councils. Theirs is the experience from which we learn and theirs is the future we try to secure.

Ethiopian Women Co-operate to Farm

Shone Arero belongs to a peasant association in the Tuka Co-operative in Southern Ethiopia. Through the Freedom from Hunger Campaign of FAO, Christian Aid provides funds for credit and training for women farmers to help them to produce more food around the home. Animals or cash loans are given to the women, which they repay after three years. Shone explains what the project has done:

"It's hot, and we don't have big trees in our area. We have more animals than crops, and we settle in an area for seven or eight years and then move on. I have been in my present house for the past nine years. Even when we're settled, most of the time the men and boys go in search of grass and water for the animals, while we wives and children stay at home.

Our Co-operative was founded three years ago. We were told of its importance and we paid two Birr (about 60 pence) for the registration, but it was only after two years that I understood that it is really important. It is like a mother with her children. It offers many services, for example, sugar, salt and clothes from the Co-operative shop. We had no way of getting these things before.

Shone Arero (right), Tuka Co-operative, Ethiopia.

From the Co-operative, I got a goat a year ago. The first goat died from disease, but I got another from the insurance money. It has had three kids since then, which aren't big enough to sell yet. I want to build up the herd, selling only the male goats.

Women have started joining in development programmes and meetings – before this, we only collected wood and did housework. The most important thing now is water. We need it for animals and people. This affects women more because we have to walk such a long way to get water. We can't farm if we have to spend so much time looking for water."

No Farming without Water

Mali

Many of the projects supported by Christian Aid in Africa and India aim to improve village water supplies for crops, animals and household use. At Bandiagara on the rocky and drought-affected Dogon plateau in Mali, the Catholic Mission has for more than 15 years helped villagers with well-digging, boreholes and small dams. Since Christian Aid started funding this work in the mid-1970s, wells have been dug at 205 sites in 173 villages. Nearly all the digging and lining of wells is done by the villagers themselves; much of the Christian Aid funds is spent on explosives to blast a way through the rock.

The Bandiagara well-digging project in Mali has saved lives and kept farmers on the land.

Villagers have also built small dams to conserve what little surface water there is and are now able to grow potatoes, onions, aubergines and mango and papaya trees. "For some villages," says Father Yves of the Mission, "it's a question of life or death. Without wells, boreholes and dams, the Dogon Plateau would have been emptied of people. Through the programme numerous human lives are being saved and the suffering of thousands of women is alleviated."

Somalia
After drought in north-east Somalia in 1985-6, the Ecumenical Development Group for Somalia, a team of Somali mechanics supported by European church agencies, was asked to re-equip water supply points for the nomads who

keep animals in the region. These are some of Africa's driest rangelands, where camels, goats, sheep and cattle outnumber people and where meat and milk provide the main food.

For two years the church agencies helped the mechanics to repair and replace water pumps. The programme is now helping to install new solar pumps, supported by mobile workshops, and to train local people to operate and repair them. Solar pumps overcome the problems of breakdown and fuel supply which have beset diesel pumps. Large numbers of evenly spread water supply points prevent overgrazing by livestock around the pumps. The elders of the community run the programme, and charges for water supplies and spare parts will ensure that it becomes self-financing during the 1990s.

Kenya

"I am happy that I now have green vegetables, which will keep my family healthy. When I was getting water from the dam, it was taking me three hours. Now I save time and have more time to work on the vegetable garden." Susan Wanjiku is from one of the farming families resettled on the dry ranchlands of Laikipia in Kenya's Rift Valley. Families like hers asked the National Council of Churches to help them dig and line sunken water tanks, each holding between 10,000 and 30,000 gallons of rainwater. The water from the 112 tanks now built is used to boost home vegetable production and impressive results have been achieved. Susan has had her tank since 1986 and has grown kale, tomatoes, spinach and onions. She has also been able to sell some of her vegetables and from the income bought a goat.

Christian Aid has financed the tank construction and is now supporting a new programme to add covers to the tanks as well as helping farmers' groups in the area clean up and improve 15 earth dams. The work is within reach of the churches' centre which trains the families in nutrition, primary health care, soil and water conservation, tree-planting and dryland farming.

Survival on the Drylands

In the arid lands of north-east Brazil, the poor survive in an environment that is physically and economically hostile. Every year thousands give up the struggle and take their few belongings to swell the ranks of shanty-town dwellers in the cities. The combined effect of chronic drought, burning sun and constant winds is to dry out and loosen the topsoil.

When the infrequent rains fall – and they fall heavily – the topsoil is washed away.

But farmers can counter the effects of the weather by terracing the land, digging ditches or building stone walls. Beans can be planted along the divides to provide windbreaks. Many farmers in the North-East have teamed up in rural workers' unions to carry out such work and increase their production.

At Campina Grande farmers have found an organisation prepared to listen to their needs and help them consider ways forward. The Programme for Appropriate Community Technology (PATAC) of the Redemptorist Congregation – a Christian Aid partner – provides that service through its experience of dryland farming.

"The soil is exhausted; it's become a mixture of sand and stones," Brother Urbano, PATAC's co-ordinator, points out. The answer is to make organic compost from material like maize stalks, straw and leaves. Rather than spread it over the land, he recommends putting it only in the seed or plant hole. "This way farmers can get a better harvest and bigger production of organic material for future use."

The PATAC team is also on hand to discuss with farmers the best crops to plant. Maize is the most common crop but, according to Brother Urbano, it needs a lot of water: "Sunflower, sesame and sorghum do well without rain." These crops can be used as animal feed, but cattle-raising has its problems. "Cattle eat all the organic material on the land – small animals are better." Farmers in touch with PATAC have used the market intelligently. Raising small animals like chickens, ducks, pigs, goats and sheep provides a better income than selling maize to a middle-man at harvest time when prices are low.

Fortunes Turned by Trees and Terracing

Osman Ali Idris is a semi-nomadic farmer on the Rora-Habab plateau in Eritrea. He scratches a living from the wheat and barley he grows in his sloping, stony fields. In the 1984 drought he lost two-thirds of his animals. "The trees are dying," he says, "and more and more soil is being washed away, leaving the hillsides bare."

With the help of a project supported by Christian Aid, Osman and his neighbours have started to reverse the effects of drought and soil erosion. "From January to April," he explains, "we work in groups of 10 farmers, building stone terraces across our fields. In May and June we plant trees on the slopes above our fields." After only two years, the terraces have begun to prove their worth. Soil is being trapped on the upper sides, the rainwater sinks in and the yields of grain in the terraced fields have almost doubled. The farmers receive seeds, tools, training and food-for-work from the project but no artificial fertilisers are used.

Village assemblies have agreed strict controls on cutting live trees and are well aware of the dangers of deforestation. At courses run by the project, the most controversial issue is grazing control. Farmers who saw their herds halved in the drought do not believe their reduced herds can be damaging the environment. Others like Osman have watched the goats eating young trees and sheep digging grass roots out of the ground. Ironically, the five much-needed dams which the project is building may increase the pressure on grazing land by encouraging families and animals to stay on the plateau during the dry season, when they used to be in the habit of migrating in search of water. The design of the dams and the use of the water are being carefully planned to overcome this problem.

The 12,000 people on the Rora-Habab plateau are seeing the first signs of recovery but many labour-intensive projects of this kind will be needed if the loss of soil and water from the Ethiopian highlands is to be reversed, making famine a thing of the past.

Christian Aid/Martin Whiteside

"The trees are dying." The landscape Osman faced in Eritrea before he began terracing and tree-planting.

The Salt of the Earth

"As a town Damulog's days were numbered. It would become a dead town if nothing was done to prevent soil erosion." That was the future when Christian Aid partner Romeo Tiongco arrived in 1974 as a parish priest. A market town in the southern Philippine island of Mindanao, Damulog lies amid hills which over 90 percent of the 12,600 inhabitants are farming.

After years in which only maize has been grown, much of the soil has been exhausted and steadily eroded by heavy tropical rainfall. 64-year-old Alejandro Nunez said that his land, which once produced 60 cavans (50 kg sacks) of maize per hectare, harvested only 10-15 cavans per hectare in 1984. 16 families left Damulog because they could not make a living on the land they had.

Started by a group of local farmers with the help of Romeo Tiongco, the Damulog Community Organisation sent some of its members to a local agricultural institute for training in Sloping Agricultural Land Technology, or SALT. The farmers returned equipped to show others these methods for rehabilitating their land. The key to SALT is the ipil-ipil tree. This tree grows quickly from seed and its leaves are a good fertiliser.

Alejandro joined other farmers in marking out contour lines along a steep hillside using an A-shaped wooden frame with a stone hanging down as a plumb-line. They then planted a double row of ipil-ipil trees to retain the soil. The terraces in between will be planted with alternating crops, including mung beans and maize, to protect the earth from exhaustion by a single crop. Farmers who terraced their land in this way three years ago have already increased their harvests and their incomes.

Home Processing in Paraguay

Peasants in Paraguay, like rural people elsewhere, get the worst of the market system: low, unstable income from the products they sell, rising prices for what they buy. Farming families in three districts of the North-East have formed local groups of basic Christian communities, with 10-15 families in each group. The groups have questioned the official policy of emphasising cash crops and have sought help to produce more food for their own needs. This includes maize, cassava, beans, peanuts, pumpkins, sweet potatoes and sugar cane, though each family still has a small plot for cash crops like rice, cotton or yerba mate (Paraguayan tea) to be traded between the districts.

Through the Disciples of Christ Friendship Mission, Christian Aid has given the groups a grant for basic equipment: disc ploughs, carts, nine vegetable oil presses and three multi-purpose diesel mills. The presses, designed by a workshop in Paraguay to extract oil from peanuts, enable the families to avoid buying expensive vegetable oil from outside. The multi-purpose mills are used for rice husking and making flour from maize and cassava, and have proved popular with over a thousand families. The grant also covers the building of three community stores to sell necessities like rice, flour, soap and tools and to help the three districts to exchange their surplus goods.

The families now benefit from their own small-scale processing facilities and can increase their trade in local food products. But production – whether for consumption or for sale – is not the main object. Above all, the peasants' organisations are being strengthened to help them tackle the many problems they share.

Indian Women make Dairying Pay

By persevering, a group of poor women can make a real success of a dairy co-operative. This is the lesson learned by Christian Aid's partner CHAD in the south Indian state of Tamil Nadu. CHAD is the Community Health and Development Department of the Christian Medical College and Hospital at Vellore, which formed a dairying co-op exclusively for women in the village of Sathumadurai.

CHAD's health workers realised that young women needed gainful employment to overcome their poverty. The women formed a Madar Sangam (women's group) and, after first receiving help with handicrafts, convinced CHAD that dairying would be viable. Less than a quarter of the households in the village owned milch animals, but the women's co-op helped its 85 members to obtain more. It assists women with bank loans to purchase animals, provides a steady market for milk at a standard price, supervises loan repayment by deductions from members' fortnightly milk payments and buys feed in bulk to distribute to members. The co-op now shows a steady profit and has built a room to keep equipment, records and animal feed. A family with an animal, after repaying the loan and paying for feed, can earn on average 75-100 rupees (£3-£4) per month.

Muniamma is a farm labourer who owns no land and was

deserted by her husband. Her two sons are masons and, with her daughter, she relies on their earnings and her own from farm work. With a bank loan, she bought a buffalo in 1983 which has now calved, and in 1984 was able to buy another cow which gives four litres of milk per day. Muniamma buys one cart of hay every six months for 150 rupees. She also buys local concentrate feeds and collects green fodder and sugar cane waste from the fields.

The Sathumadurai co-op has shown that women need credit for buying animals and feed, land to grow fodder, veterinary care and training in improved dairying. It has also proved that dairying can be made to pay even for households with little or no land and that illiterate villagers can run a dairy programme on their own. The co-op convinced CHAD of the value of directing its programmes towards women.

Preparing for the Lean Years

When Zimbabwe fell victim to severe drought from 1982-4, some farmers turned to the churches for help in making up their food shortage. At first Christian Care, the churches' development agency, helped with relief supplies, but soon decided to take a leaf out of the book of Genesis and learn from Joseph's story in building up local food stocks as a protection against the lean years. From 1985 it launched a programme to reinforce the farmers' ability to produce their own food – Operation Joseph was born.

In the Malindi co-operative vegetable garden in the dry province of Matabeleland, Marita Dube works tirelessly for her family and the co-op. With five children and ten grandchildren, she knows the value of the improved vegetable production, "Before we had the vegetables the children seemed to be stunted in their growth. Now we see a marked change."

The garden became possible when the co-op members obtained a diesel engine to pump water from a nearby river. They asked Christian Care for help with pipes, fencing and seeds. Christian Care, "gave us every implement from the fence to the gardening tools," Marita explains. Now the co-op is able to sell some of its tomatoes and cabbages to other local families, and use the proceeds to meet expenses like fuel and ploughing for the maize which its members grow. Some of the co-op members left when a food-for-work programme was started in the area, but they were expected to return once the food hand-outs ended.

With support from agencies like Christian Aid, Christian Care is helping farmers throughout Zimbabwe with seeds, fertilisers, cattle, tools and water sources like wells, boreholes and small dams. Operation Joseph is proving that, just with small supplies of inputs, the poorest families in the driest areas can grow the food they need to stay healthy.

Now the Sea gives us a Living

In fishing as well as in farming, the benefits can go either to the rich or to the poor. Developing countries needing foreign exchange often reach export agreements with big industrial fishing fleets from the developed world. But coastal fisheries can provide both food and jobs for poor people. One country which has tried to encourage its small-scale fishermen is Nicaragua.

El Astillero is a small bay of breathtaking beauty on the Pacific coast, 100 miles south of Managua. But its beauty hides poverty. In 1983 18 fishermen in one co-operative eked out a living from home-made canoes. One of them, Orlando, explains, "Before the co-op was founded there were only a few small boats with paddles here." Now there are four co-ops with 97 members and a fishing centre built by INPESCA, Nicaragua's fishing board. The centre has space for processing and a refrigerated store, and INPESCA supplies the fishermen on credit with boats, outboard motors, fuel and nets.

Red snappers, lobsters, sharks and eels caught by the fishermen find a ready market in the capital, Managua. But marketing depended on a single refrigerated lorry which worked 18 hours per day, seven days per week, to transport the catch. So Christian Aid has helped to overcome the bottlenecks in storage and transport by financing a new five-tonne lorry, a refrigeration unit and an ice-making machine. It is also important that the government should maintain prices for its fishermen and farmers which encourage them to produce.

Co-ops like those at El Astillero help both the national economy – fish is a good, cheap source of protein – and the fishing families involved. The project will eventually provide 200 jobs in fishing and processing. As Orlando adds, "Now the sea gives us a living, though the life is still tough."

Fiona Macintosh

Fish processing on the shore at El Astillero, Nicaragua: with improved equipment, the fishing families' income will be more secure.

CHAPTER TEN

Small Farmers: the Role of Governments

"Most developing nations need more effective incentive systems to encourage production, especially of food crops. In short, the 'terms of trade' need to be turned in favour of the small farmer. Food security requires attention to questions of distribution, since hunger often arises from lack of purchasing power rather than lack of available food. It can be furthered by land reforms, and by policies to protect vulnerable subsistence farmers, pastoralists, and the landless – groups who by the year 2000 will include 220 million households. Their greater prosperity will depend on integrated rural development that increases work opportunities both inside and outside agriculture."

(*From One Earth to One World:* An Overview by the World Commission on Environment and Development, the Brundtland Commission.)

This book has tried to show that hunger is caused not by overall food shortage but by lack of the means to grow or buy it: lack of land or money. Simply increasing national food production does not solve the problem. The poorest families

Resources are needed most of all by small farmers

need the means to produce food or the money to buy it. Because the majority of people in the poorest countries work on the land, resources are needed most of all by small farmers, so that their food production and their incomes will increase at the same time. We have repeatedly seen that small farmers, individually and in organisations, have taken the initiative. Christian Aid's partners in the Third World have been able to assist a few, pointing the way. But they have to operate within a framework set by national and international policy, and there is a great deal that governments can do to release constraints and to help actively.

The following are actions for which Third World governments carry the main responsibility, but they apply also to governments in the North because they indicate the type of aid programmes or other policies which might help.

Increasing food and incomes for the poor

- Land reform is needed to redistribute resources to the powerless and to women. This would produce an immediate shift in priority towards food production. Land tenure must be secure so that farmers are encouraged to invest and think of future generations.
- Governments should focus support and investment on increasing the incomes of small farmers in low-resource areas. Their type of farming is based on traditional knowledge and staple foods. It is commonly rainfed, organic, sustainable and often carried out by women.
- Governments should strengthen and listen to farmers' and women's organisations.
- Farmers should become more actively involved in research, which should also give greater attention to traditional staples.
- More training of farmers should be provided, especially by and for women.
- There should be more low-cost credit schemes, not confined to richer farmers or to men.
- Governments should work to reduce post-harvest losses through help to local storage schemes and to the processing of local foods.
- Governments should set more favourable and stable producer prices for farmers' crops.

Integrating town and country

- Governments should restore the capacity of rural producers to supply the towns, in order to lessen dependence on food imports. Governments should adopt internal food policies which encourage demand for local crops.
- In order to provide a cushion while raising prices, governments need to target food subsidies to the poorest urban consumers.
- Improved roads, transport and infrastructure are essential to the marketing of small farmers' produce.
- The roles of the public and private sectors in marketing are complementary. The state needs to provide for vulnerable groups and marginal areas not served by private traders.
- Governments should give more support to local production of farm inputs and reduce dependence on imports.

Broader policies

- In the debate about export crops or food crops, the key questions are 'Who benefits?' and 'Is there the right balance between cash crops and food crops?' Moreover, because of the over-supply of many export crops, falling commodity prices and substitution of those crops by new products in the North, a policy which benefits the poor is likely to emphasise domestic food crops, not export-led agriculture.
- Where food self-sufficiency cannot be achieved at national level, governments should aim at regional food security, where necessary protecting regional markets against cheap food imports.
- More attention should be given to the concept of 'food insurance' and to the development of regional capacities for food purchase, to be used in times of shortage.

There are other measures for which Northern governments, including those in the European Community, are mainly responsible. Sometimes this responsibility is fulfilled through international agencies, some of which have been described in this book.

The policy suggestions which follow are most relevant to EC governments but many apply also to other governments in the North and to international agencies.

Northern agricultural policy

- Farm policy reforms in the North should cut over-production to reduce competition with Third World farmers, and not simply save money by dumping surpluses on world markets.
- Permanent machinery should be set up in the European Commission to examine the effects of the CAP, and all changes proposed to it, on developing countries.

Trade in food

- All major producers should phase out export subsidies and reduce production of surplus commodities which depress world prices. Exporting should not be allowed below the costs of production in the exporting countries. Minimum world reference prices should be established. Trade agreements should support the use of quantity controls such as production quotas. In the EC dairy quotas have been the most successful means of cutting production and this method should be considered for products like cereals.
- To meet the rising price of imported food, member countries of GATT should plan transitional forms of compensation for the poorest consumers in low-income,

food-importing countries. Increased aid to agriculture, food aid and trade concessions may form part of this compensation.
- Trade agreements should recognise the right of every developing country to decide its own level of food self-sufficiency and food security. Developing countries should keep their right to impose anti-dumping measures, including border controls and taxes on cheap food imports.
- The EC should improve access to its markets by developing countries, in particular reducing tariffs on processed farm products and guaranteeing access to tropical products and products like fruit and vegetables which compete with the CAP.

Food aid
- Because of the dubious value of dairy food aid, the opportunity offered by the reduction in surpluses of dairy products should be taken to bring it to an end.
- Food aid budgets for cereals need to remain, but with a stated preference for local or regional supplies (triangular operations), to stimulate trade in Third World staple foods.
- Food aid should not be used to legitimise IMF austerity programmes. If aid is to be used as a cushion, it should be alongside policies which are based on meeting human need rather than commercial or international financial interests.

Broader northern policies with an impact on food
- Northern governments must show greater political will to solve the problem of Third World debt, a double burden on the poor through cuts in social services and export-led farm policies.
- Donor influence should be more effectively applied to secure land reform, by linking aid directly to a programme of redistribution.
- Northern governments should take more active steps towards solving regional conflicts. As a first step, they should end their own promotion of arms sales.
- Governments should resist legislation which offers to multinational companies monopoly control through patents of seeds and genetic resources.
- More harmonisation is needed within Northern governments between their aid and other policies (agriculture, trade, debt, disarmament and regulation of the private sector).

The greatest contribution which many developing country governments could make to ending hunger is land reform. This is crucial for Asia, which has the largest numbers of hungry people, and for Latin America. Even in developing countries which are able to feed themselves, unequal distri-

Land and debt are the two greatest injustices postponing an end to hunger today

bution of resources prevents the poor from growing or buying enough food. Yet the Third World is held in the vice of the international economy, stifling growth and initiative and squeezing resources northwards. To create the conditions for greater equity in the Third World, the greatest contribution which Northern governments could make is to resolve the debt crisis. This is crucial for Africa, which has the most desperate hunger, and again for Latin America. Land and debt are the two greatest injustices postponing an end to hunger today. Knowing this helps us to act, for, in the words of Frances Moore Lappe and Joseph Collins:

"If we believe that famines are caused by nature's vagaries, we will feel helpless and excused from action. Learning that famines result from human-made forces, we discover hope."

Bibliography

Rhiannon Barker: **The Efficacy of the Use of Dried Skimmed Milk Powder in Food Aid Operations,** MSc Nutrition thesis, 1987.

Brundtland Commission: **From One Earth to One World, an Overview,** 1987.

Catholic Institute for International Relations: **Comment on the CAP,** 1986.

Catholic Institute for International Relations: **CAP Briefings,** 1987-8.

Robert Chambers: **Rural Development – Putting the Last First,** Longman, 1983.

Marty Chen, Manoshi Mitra, Geeta Athreya, Anila Dholakia, Preeta Law and Aruna Rao: **Indian Women,** Shakti Books.

Churches' Drought Action in Africa: Report on **The Root Causes of Hunger and Food Insufficiency in Africa,** 1985.

CILSS/Club du Sahel: **Final Recommendations of the Conference on Cereals Policies in Sahel Countries,** 1986.

Commission of the European Communities: **Food Security Policy – Examination of Recent Experiences in sub-Saharan Africa,** Commission staff paper, 1988.

Commission of the European Communities: **The Agricultural Situation in the Community – 1988 Report.**

Belinda Coote: **The Hunger Crop,** Oxfam, 1987.

Bertrand Delpeuch: **L'Enjeu Alimentaire Nord-Sud,** Editions Syros, 1987.

Pauline Eccles: **Women and Food Matters,** discussion document for the EC-NGO General Assembly, 1989.

European Parliament: **Report of the Committee of Inquiry into Agricultural Stocks,** 1987.

Food and Agriculture Organisation: **Principles of Surplus Disposal,** 1980.

Food and Agriculture Organisation: **Food Aid in Figures 1987.**

Sean J. Healy and Brigid Reynolds: **Ireland Today – Reflecting in the Light of the Gospel,** 1985.

Frances Moore Lappé and Joseph Collins: **World Hunger – 12 Myths,** Grove Press, New York, 1988.

Alan Matthews: **The CAP and the Less Developed Countries,** Gill and Macmillan, 1985.

Adrian Moyes: **Common Ground,** Oxfam, 1987.

National Consumer Council: **Consumers and the Common Agricultural Policy,** 1988.

J. H. Parotte, Executive Director, International Wheat Council: **World Trade in Cereals – Prospects for Developing Countries,** 1987.

Adria Pittock: **Animal Feeds and their Sources,** VSO, 1988.

Philip Raikes: **Modernising Hunger,** Catholic Institute for International Relations, Heinemann and James Currey, 1988.

Colin Stoneman (editor): **Zimbabwe's Prospects,** Macmillan, 1988.

United Nations: **World Survey on the Role of Women and Development,** 1985.

World Bank: **Poverty and Hunger,** 1986.

World Development Movement: **Crisis in the Sugar Industry,** 1987.

World Development Movement: **Beyond 1992,** 1989.

World Food Programme: **Annual Report,** 1987.

World Food Programme: **Food Aid Policies and Programmes,** 1989.